Edwin Roper Martin

The Rule of the Pope-King, Weighed by Facts and Figures

A Letter to the Legislators of Great Britain

Edwin Roper Martin

The Rule of the Pope-King, Weighed by Facts and Figures
A Letter to the Legislators of Great Britain

ISBN/EAN: 9783743410589

Manufactured in Europe, USA, Canada, Australia, Japa

Cover: Foto ©Lupo / pixelio.de

Manufactured and distributed by brebook publishing software
(www.brebook.com)

Edwin Roper Martin

The Rule of the Pope-King, Weighed by Facts and Figures

THE

RULE OF THE POPE-KING,

WEIGHED BY FACTS AND FIGURES.

A LETTER

To the Legislators of Great Britain.

BY

EDWIN ROPER MARTIN,

(Priest of the Diocese of Shrewsbury; some time scholar at the Roman College.)

"The integrity of the Roman States ought to be considered as the essential element of the political independence of the Italian Peninsula."—*Dispatch of Lord Palmerston to Lord Ponsonby*, September 11, 1840.

"Their temporal dominion is now confirmed by the reverence of a thousand years, and their noblest title is the free choice of a people whom they had redeemed from slavery."—*Gibbon's " Decline and Fall of the Roman Empire,"* chap. xlviii.

LONDON:

R. WASHBOURNE, 18A, PATERNOSTER ROW.

1871.

INDEX OF AUTHORITIES.

To avoid making this Pamphlet too large, by giving references on each page, the principal authorities for the statements made in it are here given *en masse*.

Gosselin, Temporal Power of the Popes. Vol. I., Chapter i. and Introduction.

Histoire des Etats de l'Eglise. Leipsic, 1860.

Etudes Statistiques sur Rome, par le Comte de Tournon, 1831.

Almanacco Romano, 1859.

Annuario Pontificio, 1867, 1870.

Civiltà Cattolica, Feb. 17, 1859.

Despatch of the Comte de Rayneval, May, 1856.

Statistics of the Ministries of Finance and Commerce, 1855, 1857-8.

Conte Della Torre on the Pontifical Finances, 1859.

Answer to Marchese Pepoli on the same subject, 1858.

Guizot. Memoires pour servir à l'Histoire, Vol. II., especially pp. 439, 441—444.

Miley's History of the States of the Church.

Revue Contemporaine, Aug, 1856.

Le Constitutionel, Aug. 12, Aug. 22, 1856.

Donovan's Rome, Vol. III.

Memorie de' nostri Tempi, Turin, 1856—1865.

The Pontifical Administration, by M. de Valdepenas, Paris, 1863.

Risposta à Liverani, Roma, 1861.

Odd Numbers of the Giornale di Roma, Unità Cattolica of Turin,
  Civiltà Cattolica of Rome, &c.

Many Private Notes made Personally in Rome.

Statistical Returns of Different Years.

Motu Proprios, of many Popes, notably those of Pius VI., Pius VII.,
  Leo XII., Gregory XVI., and Pius IX.

Thom's Statistics ; National Encyclopedia ; Almanach de Gotha.

For reasons sufficiently clear, I have not made use of Mr. Maguire's
  very important work on Rome.

The writer of this Pamphlet wishes unhesitatingly to
declare that, if anything in it is considered objectionable
by his ecclesiastical superiors, he forthwith condemns it.

THE RULE OF THE POPE-KING.

My Lords and Gentlemen,

  You are the law-givers of a great nation; you
are at the same time the keepers of the national conscience
and its voice. You cannot be careless whether justice or injustice is done in the outside world : the national conscience
must judge of the right or the wrong of the public acts of
other nations; you have to direct that judgment as well as
to give utterance to it. Injustice is very contagious; you
cannot, therefore, throw off the duty of looking closely into
the great public acts of other nations; because the national
conscience, which you have to keep, may catch the deadly
disease of a false measure of justice, and the national mind
may so grow corrupt. You were at the pains to look closely
into the acts by which Poland was wronged, those by which
Denmark was wronged, and those by which Hanover was
wronged. Another great national act is before you to-day;
you have to look at its justice or its injustice, and to accept
it as a just act or to protest against it as a great crime. For
every national act must be the one or the other; and when
it is not a just act, it must be a crime to its neighbour or to
itself.

  Human society is linked together by certain laws. There
could be no society without such links, because, unless the

rights of individuals and of communities were defined, and then hedged in by laws, the different aggregates of the human family would be in a state of perpetual conflict. All human laws have a common basis—the moral law, that is, the notions of right and wrong webbed in with our very humanity. It is the business of legislators to take up the threads of this moral law, and to make rules for the individual or for the society. So again, the public conscience is only the aggregate of the private consciences of the state ; and it is the aggregate of public consciences which makes the great universal conscience. In order to hold together any society of men it is necessary to make public laws ; and in order to hold together the great human family it was necessary to make international laws. If a man cannot break the moral law—as it affects his individual conscience—and keep his self-respect ; if a nation becomes a discredit to the world when the laws between man and man are of no account in it ; surely it is equally true that the entire human society and each collective portion of human society must suffer when the international laws are broken by any nation in its dealings with another, or when they are left in abeyance, or to take care of themselves. For if the internal security of a nation consists in the observance of its laws, surely, its real external security comes from the proper observance of laws between nation and nation.

Pius IX.—the Sovereign of Rome—has lost his sovereignty. It has been taken from him, not by his people—for a plebiscitum after an armed invasion, and registered by the invaders, can have no place in the judgment of the fact—but by a neighbouring nation. It has been taken from him in time of peace, without aggression on his part. Not even a moral aggression on his part could be made out of the fact that he continued to protest—in words only—against the similar seizure of a previous portion of his territories. Nor was there any moral aggression in the fact that he gave an asylum to refugees from that territory, as from any other ; else Belgium, Switzerland, not to say England—the focus of

refugee plots—might more justly be invaded by any of the
great powers of Europe. This fact established, he must have
lost his crown in accordance with the principles of the law
of nations, or in violation of them; he must have lost it,
therefore, justly or unjustly. Or—as in the case of a man
dying from starvation who takes a loaf—the laws ceased to
apply to his case; his peculiar rights ceased before a tremendous necessity, as the rights of property over food cease
before another's imminent death from starvation. But, just
as for the outward acts the thief would be judged, before he
could prove his case;—so this tremendous public necessity
must be well proven in face of the world, before the act can
go unpunished by the condemnation of men.

Before looking the facts in the face, one must pray you,
my Lords and Gentlemen, to put clean aside any bias you
may have to the act or against it, from the fact that a great
religious question is mixed up with the question of the Papal
Sovereignty. The matter must be tried by the rules of pure
justice; it is not fair to try it in any other way. You may
rejoice that a great blow has been dealt at a system which
you dislike, or of which you disapprove, and therefore come
under the condemnation of those who do evil that good may
come of it. Or again, you may have a natural impatience
of acts which strike at the heart of feelings dearest to you;
but in neither case would this be to do your part as Law-
makers—as supporters of national honour and national
justice—as men who, having the interest of a nation at
heart, are bound to look to the observance of the laws
which rule the intercourse of nations with one another.

And here, at the outset of our search after justice, we are
met by the most important of all the questions raised upon
the subject: Had the dispossessed Pope-King any right to
his sovereignty? To answer it, we must go back far into
very misty ages. But misty though the ages were, there is
nothing historically clearer in them than this same Papal
Sovereignty. We can trace it right up to its source; we can
follow it as it developes, as does a mighty river from a tiny

stream. The Popes of Rome were the Bishops of Rome, before they became its Kings. They became its Bishops by their election to the seat of St. Peter, the first Bishop of Rome. As the representative of St. Peter, the Bishop of Rome had always the first place in the Christian Church. Other Bishops ruled over their dioceses; his sphere of government was the Christian world. Nobody ever disputed the succession to St. Peter, or the place of the Bishop of Rome among Bishops, till the 13th century, when a scholar of mark in his day—Marsilius, of Padua,—tried to prove that St. Peter had never been at Rome at all. His only tangible evidence was the questionable meaning of certain texts of scripture; he could find no support in antiquity; no writer of the Christian Church, not even writers most jealous of Papal interference, had given his view so much as a thought. On the other hand, St. Ignatius and St. Irenæus, disciples of the Apostles, plainly asserted the contrary; and the position of the Bishop of Rome in the Church, was built upon what no one, in any age, had dreamed of disputing. In the second century, people would come from distant parts of the world to pray at the tomb of St. Peter; and when the Church had peace, all the world turned there. Marsilius, however, had an end to serve by his boldness in contradicting the venerated belief of ages. He was chaplain to the Emperor Louis IV., in his day, the great secular rival of the power of the Popes;—and for him he even claimed the right of superintending and directing the internal discipline of the Church. If he could get men to believe that the Bishops of Rome were not the successors of St. Peter, he could disprove all the dignity and place which had grown up about them. No longer Primates of the Church, they would have no claim to an honour grounded on a false belief and an imposture; and the city of Rome, and the headship of the Church, might be claimed by the German Emperor, without any great shock to Christian feeling. It is enough to know that he proved nothing; that his scheme failed miserably; that the great Dutch Protestant Grotius has asserted that "no good

Christian ever doubted that St. Peter was at Rome ;" and that that very orthodox Anglican, Bishop Pearson, was at the pains to write a learned dissertation in defence of the same position.

We presume, then, that the Bishop of Rome fills the place of St. Peter, that the spiritual rank he has always held and still holds in the Catholic Church was founded neither upon imposition, nor upon incredulity. To allow this, is to commit oneself to nothing more than to the historical truth of the assertion, that St. Peter was at Rome, and, of what lies beside it, the assertion that he was head of the Christian Church there. For this also is affirmed, or allowed, by all ecclesiastical writers till the time of Marsilius. And since, in its struggles with the Roman Church, the Eastern Church never once disputed this standpoint, it cannot be very difficult for a man of the nineteenth century to admit it, even though he may refuse to admit what Catholics call its consequences, just as the Eastern Church does. For though Marsilius might have lighted on an historical truth as Copernicus lighted upon his solar theory, yet the starting point of an historical truth, and the starting point of a solar theory, are things of a widely different nature—for the one starts from ignorance or error; the other from facts. Presuming then that the Bishop of Rome held the place of St. Peter, we pass on. The earlier Bishops of Rome were subject to the Emperor in all things temporal, and had, of course, as heads of a persecuted and despised sect, no honourable place in the world. All Pagan governments had acted on the counsel of their wisest men, and had accorded high place and outward surroundings to the heads of the various Pagan religions. It was natural then that Constantine, having at least a great leaning to, and faith in the Christian religion, should endeavour to exalt its hitherto despised ministers in the eyes of the people. He gave lands and treasures to the Roman Church ; and, as it was the chiefest church of the world, he made it also the wealthiest. That he had no personal ambition in this, is evident from the fact that he never interfered in spiritual things, except to assist the Bishops, if need were, to carry out their decrees. From his show of respect to Bishops of the Church, it became a custom with the Emperors to use the Bishops as almoners in works of mercy, and as justicers in redressing wrongs. When the seat of Empire was moved to Constantinople, the Bishop of Rome entered upon a still greater pomp of outward place; armed guards were put at his disposal, and the civil magistrates were ordered to back him in any difficulty he might have in the discharge of his duties of justice and mercy. It may be said that the just and blameless lives of the early Bishops of Rome, and their peculiar mode of election, made those outward dignities only natural. The answer lies in the retort—do the moral errors of hereditary kings deprive them of the civil rights conferred by choice upon their nobler forefathers ? If it be answered—they do, there is no sovereign in Europe who can sit honestly on the throne of his fathers, since in himself, or in his immediate ancestors, he has forfeited his rights of sovereignty.

The removal of the seat of Empire and the appointment of Governors for Italy—often only needy courtiers—would have brought about in Italy the same removal of the old landmarks which followed the invasions of the bar-barians everywhere else in Europe, but for the Bishops of Rome. St. Leo the Great twice saved Rome. All the world knows how he faced Attila, how he faced Gens-eric. But all the world does not know that it was the great spiritual bond between the Bishop of Rome and the Christians of the world, which kept Rome a power in the world, and which saved even lands that fell within the shadow of this great spiritual sovereignty. For, even though the waves of invasion might sweep over Rome, they always broke there, and the great resistless tide of invasion yielded to the moral power of the Bishop of Rome. The Emperors did little or nothing to help their Italian subjects; they had troubles and jealousies nearer home to attend to; the tide of invasion was not setting their way. The exarchs who governed for them at Ravenna—not at Rome, could do little with the forces at their command. It was always the same story—the only real barrier to the cruelty and rapacity of the invaders was the especially sacred character of the Bishops of Rome. St. Gregory the Great, in his day (A.D. 590), says it was often difficult for him to tell whether he was a pastor or a temporal prince, so heavily did temporal cares press on him as Bishop of Rome. We find him sending one Leontius as governor to Nepi, and ordering the people to obey Leontius as himself. We find him sending a General to Naples to command the troops there—giving orders about the defence of cities—directing the officers of the Italian army—making terms with the Lombard masters of North Italy. Under this real power, the exarchs themselves were glad to take refuge ; and there were times when even the Emperors were conscious enough of it—times such as that when Pope Vigilius could secure a constitution for the Italians, and get the rights of the Roman people to certain portions' of territory, which their Gothic conquerors had made over to them, confirmed by the Emperor.

The Empire was, however, losing ground in Italy less from invasion, than from the folly of the absent Emperor. The Italians were strongly Catholic ; the Emperors were, in most cases, either heretics or patrons of heresy. The heretical Emperors tried to propagate heresy by the mastery of might. The Catholic Italians rebelled. When the Emperor Justinian II. (A.D. 692) wanted to force the Bishop of Rome to subscribe to the decrees of an heretical council, even the Italian army rose, and secured to the Pope his personal liberty. Once again in the time of that Emperor (A.D. 701), the same army rose to protect John VI. against the abuse of imperial authority. The Roman people refused to obey the heretical governor, appointed by the Emperor Philipicus, and only tolerated him in the city at the express interference of his opponent—the Bishop. A few years later came the attack upon holy images, and the Catholic Italians washed their hands of the Empire. The Lombards sided with the Catho-

lics, and the very army forgat its old jealousy of them, and
declared its purpose to proclaim a new Imperator. The
Bishop of Rome saved Italy for the Emperor this once again.
Then the Exarch obtained new troops, bought the King of
the Lombards by a bribe of Spoleto and Benevento, and the
two together attacked the generous Bishop of Rome
(A.D. 715). Gregory II. was then Bishop; he went out to
meet the Lombard King, awed him to his knees, forgave the
Exarch, and got the Catholic troops to join him in opposing
a mushroom Emperor who had appeared in Tuscany. Gregory III., who succeeded (A.D. 731) as Bishop, began with
pleading with the Emperor, who was as zealously as ever
bent on propagating image-breaking; and won the angry
people to use the same gentle force with him. The Emperor's
reply was—a fleet sent to plunder the chief Italian cities,
and new taxes, though these were already heavy enough.
He also seized the property of the Roman Church in Sicily
and Calabria, valued at £16,000 yearly. And in this hour
of misery, the Lombards poured southward again, and Rome
was besieged.

By this time, however, a great star had risen in Western
Europe. Charles Martel—Lord Chamberlain to the kings of
the Franks—had won his great victory at Tours over the
Moors, and so saved Europe from becoming the kingdom of
Mahomet. To him, the Bishop and people of Rome naturally
turned. He was on his way to help them, when the death
of the Emperor and of the Bishop changed the state of
Italian affairs. The new Pope succeeded in getting the
Lombards to terms. They restored several cities and territories—not, indeed, to a powerless empire, but to the Roman
State. By this time, in fact, the people of Rome cared to
know no other head than their Bishop. Nor, indeed, did
many other parts of Italy—the towns of Spoleto and Rieti
had made themselves freely over to the Roman Church. But
the Bishop did not forget that he was still a subject of the
Emperor—he secured for him some of the old dominions, and
the Emperor publicly thanked him for his care, and in return

made over to the Roman Church some large tracts of territory to the south. But Bishop Zachary died (A.D. 741), and
the Lombards considered that all their contracts died with
him. The exarchate could no longer keep itself alive; the
last of the exarchs fled. The Lombards seized all central
Italy, and resolved this time to master Rome for ever. The
new Bishop—Stephen II. (A.D. 752)—tried hard to come to
terms with the Lombards; the Emperor himself urged him to
make any terms, as he could give no help; but King Astolphus had set his heart on Rome, and would make no terms
short of its possession. Then Stephen turned to King Pepin
of France, son of Charles Martel, and fled from Rome to his
court, to call in his aid the more successfully. Pepin con-
sulted his notables, and took oath with them to restore to
the Roman State the possessions which the Lombards had
seized. He first sent to ask for this restoration; and, when
it was refused, he came to Italy in person. He forced
Astolphus to create a solemn deed of conveyance of the
usurped territories, including the exarchate, to the Roman
Church and State.

When Pepin's back was turned, Astolphus broke his
promises, ravaged all Italy again, and once more sat down
before the gates of Rome. Pepin was sent for; he returned
at once. Rome had already been three months besieged;
but at the news of Pepin's arrival in Italy, Astolphus raised
the siege, and hastened northward to defend his native
Lombardy. Once more he was brought to terms; as a
penalty for his broken faith he had to include part of his
own territory in the new cession; and once more he solemnly
made over the old lands and cities to the Holy See—this
time by a solemn deed of conveyance for ever. The territory thus made over or restored, lay pretty evenly between
the Po and the Tanaro, and the Apennines and the Adriatic.
The title deeds of this property were solemnly laid on the
confession of St. Peter, in the handwriting of Astolphus, with
the keys of the twenty-three cities which returned to the rule
of the Bishop of Rome (A.D. 754). It was looked on by all the

parties concerned, as a solemn act of restitution of the parts, usurped by the Lombards from the Church and State of Rome.

From this time the Bishops of Rome—Popes or Fathers of the Christian world—have been also kings of Rome. We hear no more of the rights of the Emperors; their rights had passed with their inability to defend the people who belonged to them by the feeblest of ties—by little else, in fact, but the chivalrous feelings of adherence to the shadow of an ancient glory, and the moral sense of duty to the powers that were still nominally real, though really but shadows. The perishing people had elected a master who lived among them—a master who had proved his power to repel the fiercest kings—a master about whom fell the shadow of a divine place in the world, higher than that of the proudest Emperors. The sovereignty grew by subsequent treaties, subsequent concessions. In after difficulties, the Franks were called in—not by the Pope-Kings only, but by the Roman people, whom we find calling themselves "Faithful subjects of the Holy Church, and of Paul our Lord, the sovereign Pontiff and universal Pope." So it was that Charlemagne came to Italy, to help them against Didier, another turbulent King of the Lombards. He came, but he claimed nothing in return. It was freely, and in gratitude, that the proud name of Emperor of the Romans was given to him, and not till he had confirmed the independence of the territories of Rome, which included, in his day (A.D. 774), Parma, Mantua, Venice, Istria, and even Corsica. And his confirmation was renewed, and honoured, by those who came after him.

To carry this sketch farther would be needless. The Bishops of Rome are Kings—Kings, as we have seen, by as fair desert as any Kings or Emperors who have ever reigned. On this count, at least, my Lords and Gentlemen, all that is said against them breaks down. Pius IX. has an incontestable and sacred right to his sovereignty. But to bind together this little series of facts, no proof will be better than the words of the infidel and apostate Gibbon, who, hating the Papacy as he hated that Christianity which it served to propagate and defend and keep alive in the world, yet says of the temporal sovereignty of the Popes these eloquent words : " By the necessity of their situation, the inhabitants of Rome were cast into the rough model of a republican government; they were compelled to elect some judges in peace, and some leaders in war; the nobles assembled to deliberate, and their resolves could not be executed without the union and consent of the multitude. The style of the Roman senate and people was revived, but the spirit was fled ; and their new independence was disgraced by the tumultuous conflict of licentiousness and oppression. The want of laws could only be supplied by the influence of religion, and their foreign and domestic counsels were moderated by the authority of the Bishop. His alms, his sermons, his correspondence with the kings and prelates of the West, his recent services, their gratitude and oath, accustomed the Romans to consider him as the first magistrate or prince of the city. The Christian humility of the Pope was not offended by the name of *Dominus* or Lord ; and their face and inscription are still apparent on the most ancient coins. Their temporal dominion was now confirmed by the reverence of a thousand years; and their noblest title is the free choice of a people whom they had redeemed from slavery."—" Decline and Fall of the Roman Empire," chap. xlviii.

The Pope is a king. But there are kings who rule with rods of iron, kings who rule with reins of silk, and kings who do not rule at all, but who leave the ruling to their Ministers, while they enjoy the empty name, and the outward grandeur of sovereignty. The Papal sovereignty might have been what we call a tyranny, or it might have been so light that it was not felt at all. In truth, however, it is neither of these; it is a real sovereignty, without being tyrannical. It is also a very peculiar sovereignty, and in this peculiarity lies its safeguard from becoming merely a lifeless fossil. This peculiarity is also the best guarantee for the exercise of its power in a way most likely to help on the happiness of the people. Theoretically, then, the Papal sovereignty means this—the best and wisest is elected by the many good and wise, because he is the best and wisest. Each new sovereign is independent of the views and the practices of his predecessor, except in so far as the views and practices of each Pope must be in agreement with the laws of morality as interpreted by the Catholic Church. Each Pope comes to the throne far more independent than any hereditary monarch at his accession. More than any hereditary monarch does he feel the responsibility of a position to which he was elected for his presumed merits; and he knows that there lies on him the heavy burden of a place exposed to all the eyes of the world. He knows also that men look to him to bring to bear upon his reign the more extended light of his times, and to correct any abuses which may have crept in during the rule of his predecessors. His temporal sovereignty is not a mere appanage of a greater sovereignty; it is a sovereignty of itself, requiring in the sovereign an especial care, lest he who has the keeping of the conscience of the entire world, should himself sin against morality and the rights of justice. That this is not idle theorising is clear from the strange fact that even those Popes whose private lives fell below the high standard of the great mass of their kind, were in no case tyrannical rulers, were often noticeable for especial care of their subjects. And, indeed, it would be a strange paradox if the government, theoretically the best in the world, should, in operation, turn out to be the worst in the world. Between theory and practice there may be many misfits; but there is no such wide and complete want of proportion between them.

The character of the Papal sovereignty is monarchical— an elective absolute monarchy. But, in truth, its absolutism is so affected by the peculiarities of the manner of election, as to leave the Pope in reality little but the honoured head of a republic of statesmen. Even were it not so, there is this great distinction to be borne in mind. An hereditary absolute monarchy is generally a great evil; for where the only title to the throne is relationship to the sovereign who has last filled it, there are many chances that the successor of a good and great monarch will undo much that his predecessor ' has done for good. Where, however, the monarchy is also elective, and where the theory of election requires worth in the candidate and worth in the electors, there are many chances of a noble reign. Now the Pope-King has a special character attached to one portion of his sovereignty. He is the teacher of justice to the entire world. In these days of the world, no Pope-King could dare to give the lie to his public teaching by practice flatly opposed to it. And of Pius IX., it is almost waste of words to say that the purity of his life, and the large love of his heart, are guarantees that he, at least, has not so contradicted himself.

The character of the Papal government may be understood from an analysis of its several parts, or by considering it as it affects those who are its subjects. The first of these ways has its advantages, but it seems to me that the second has more. We will, therefore, examine the public life of a subject of the Pope-King, so as best to understand the nature of his government. For the general condition of its subjects is the true test of the worth or worthlessness of any government.

The first point in the public life of a subject is his opportunities for education. In every country, these opportunities vary, as one lives in the towns or in the country, the town education being always the superior of the two. If the higher education of the towns is, as in Scotland and in most foreign countries, within reach of country lads, from the smallness of its cost, the education of the State can hardly be considered very low—provided, of course, as we presume, that the character of this education is superior. These points conceded, we may pass in review the opportunities for instruction afforded in the dominions of the Pope-King.

2

In every commune—village or town district—of the State, there is a school. Probably there is no commune of the State which has not two schools, one for boys and one for girls, as the sexes are never mixed, except in the infant schools. The communal schools are entirely free. The expenses are borne altogether by the commune, or by the commune assisted by government grants. The master—for the mistress will generally be a religious of some sort—is chosen by a local board, after examination in its presence. If he passes, he is elected for two years, with a right to re-election if the board approves of his school management and moral conduct during that period. If he considers that he has been arbitrarily deposed, he can appeal to the Delegate, or governor of the province, who is bound to hear both sides of the question. These schools are under the inspection of the mayor and of a diocesan inspector.

This school machinery is, however, the mere skeleton of the education which is offered, even in less known parts of the State. For there will be in many communes, certainly there will be in all towns and cities, one or more religious bodies of men or women whose special work is teaching, and who will therefore offer their quota to the tale. In the towns and cities, there are also private schools for both girls and boys. These cannot be opened, as in England, by any body who takes a fancy to earn a respectable livelihood by the profession of a teacher. Any one who wishes to set up a school, must first procure a certificate of confidence, from a Board appointed by the Bishop of the diocese in which the commune is situated. To this Board he must bring certificates of unblemished moral reputation, and of good health—which last testimonial might with advantage be demanded from many private-school teachers in our country, where bile and bad health colour falsely a very important work. Only sixty pupils are allowed under one teacher ; if there are more, an assistant must be employed.

The Jesuits, the Fathers of The Pious Schools, the Benedic-

tines, and the Sommaschi Fathers, have institutions in different parts of the State, and offer to their pupils the higher
branches of education. And the State has eight Universities
and two quasi-Universities, each with its staff of Professors
elected from eminent members of each faculty. Two pounds
a year would more than cover the expenses of education at
any one of them, and at one of them the education is
entirely free. From statistics taken just before the break-up
of the State by the first invasion, the numbers attending the
classes at seven of these Universities amounted to 13,435.
At the Universities and quasi-Universities together, the figure
must have exceeded sixteen thousand.

To pass, however, to the state of education in the city of
Rome. On this point, I may be allowed to call into court
some statistics made by myself, when residing at Rome four
years ago, and to make use of other well-proven statistics in
my possession. In Rome, then, there are infant schools.
Those most strictly such, which receive children from the
ages of three to five, and give them freely a mid-day meal,
are three in number—one in each of the poorest districts of
the city. My statistics give 372 children as attending these
three schools. The girls' schools of Rome which come next
in order, are the schools of—

The Pious Workers—eleven schools;
The Pious Mistresses—two schools;
The Ursuline Nuns—one school;
The Philipine Nuns—one school;
The Sisters of the Most Precious Blood—three schools;
The Sisters of St. Joseph—two schools;
The Sisters of Charity—one school;
The Sisters of St. Joseph—one school;
The Sister of St. Dorothy—one school;
The Sisters of Providence—one school;
The Religious of Providence—one school;
The Daughters of Providence—two schools;
The Sisters of the Sacred Heart—three schools;
The Sisters of St. Andrew—one school;

2—2

The Daughters of Charity—one school ;
The Daughters of the Sacred Heart—one school.
The average of attendance in these different schools is
5,694. They are all *free*. The course in all includes writing,
spelling, reading, ciphering, elementary history and geography, catechism, and various kinds of needle-work. Some
extend their course to Italian reading and French. A girl
with talent is never at a loss for higher education at any of
them ; as the Religious are sure to include some of superior
education. Several of these institutions take boarders, who
are educated quite apart. Before, however, looking at these
boarding-schools, it would be as well to notice the Pontifical
schools—established by Pope Alexander VII. in 1655. For
girls, there are nineteen of these. The mistresses are chosen
by a Board, presided over by the Cardinal Vicar and the Almoner for the time being. The average varies ; one of my returns gives about one thousand as a fair average for the whole
twenty-two Pontifical schools, including three for boys.
These, again, are all *free*. There are also parish schools in
several of the parishes, under the parish priest ; but these
are seldom flourishing, as the competition of better education, equally free, is so great. They are rather substitutes,
where others are in weak force. And lastly there are the
Regionary schools—my notes give 304 of these,* kept by
mistresses licensed after examination, whose charge varies
from two and a half to four francs a month. The more pre-
tentious of these offer French and music ; the others all the
usual elementary subjects, with needlework always. Six
thousand girls were attending these schools, when I made
my note. Some of these would be very young—few I
imagine, would be over fourteen. At all these schools above
mentioned, the hours are pretty much alike—from eight till
half-past eleven in the morning, and over three hours of the
afternoon. Most of the girls' schools have no holidays but
those of the Church, and a few odd days in October.

* An exhaustive description of Rome, bearing date 1864, gives 6150
as the number of girls attending these schools—then 320 in number.
The schools and the scholars would, of course, alike, fluctuate much.

The female boarding schools of Rome are always convent schools. The chief of them is in the Convent of the Sacred Heart, Trinità dei Monti, where from sixty to eighty girls of good birth are educated at a rate of about £40 a-year. Among the teachers are a French lady of Imperial birth, and some noble Scotch and Irish ladies. The education at this convent school is of the highest order in female education. The other boarding schools, professedly such, number seventeen. The more important of these are the School of the Oblate Nuns at Tor de'Speechi, for girls of noble birth; that of the Carmelites of the Barberini, also for girls of good birth; and that of the Sisters of Sant Antonio and of Sta. Susanna, who receive middle-class girls. The course, in all these schools, includes French and music, in some of them German and English. The school fees vary from £1 10s. to £2 15s. a month, washing included. The pupils all wear a uniform. There are no vacations. The maximum of pupils at any of these schools may be put at sixty; the minimum at twenty.

To pass to the schools for boys. The parish schools had 600 boys on the books, when the present Pope began his reign. In the populous quarter of the Monti, there are three Pontifical schools for boys. Of the number attending these I have no reliable statistics; but the schools are there, and in action. The Brothers of Mercy teach 300 boys at their school in the Borgo. The instruction they give is not only entirely free; they find every single article required in the schools, and they add drawing to the usual elementary studies. The Fathers of the Pious Schools, who are generally priests, have two schools in the more populous quarters —average of both, 380. The Fathers of Christian Doctrine have also two schools in crowded districts—average, 350. In one of these schools the education is carried up to Rhetoric—the reading of Latin and Italian classics, including the more difficult authors. In all these four schools Latin is taught, and in the schools of the Fathers of the Pious Schools, the higher classical teaching is offered. The Brothers of the Christian Schools—all laymen—have seven schools, lying remote from each other, which are attended by an average of over 2,000 boys. These schools are very popular; they turn out good scholars, and charge nothing. In the upper classes, Latin and Italian classics are taught. In one of these schools, there is a special class for drawing of all kinds, and another special class for singing. Boys can attend these special classes without attending the ordinary school work. These schools offer all the usual branches of commercial education, and they are conducted on what is called the Madras system—that of our national schools, which system they, in fact, originated ages before Dr. Bell or national schools were heard of.

Next to these valuable free schools may be placed the Regionary Schools for boys. At this moment there are forty-nine of these, looked after by a Diocesan Board, before which the masters are examined and licensed, under conditions and restrictions similar to those of the Regionary Mistresses. My own statistics give 3,806 as the number in attendance at these schools. They teach for six hours a day, except on Feast Days and Apostles' Days, and during the month of October. The fees vary from two francs to five francs, according to the subjects taught. The instruction includes Latin, and, in many cases, French.

Before carrying our enquiry higher, it will be useful to give a glance at two other kinds of common schools flourishing in the city of Rome. The night schools of Rome have been in full operation for the last half century. There are ten of these, and they instruct, by my own statistics, 2,000 boys. They are under the supervision of a Board, made up of the Head Teachers in various schools, and presided over by a Prelate of eminence in the Pontifical Court. Those who teach in them form also a society, which bears the whole expense of these schools; and the members of this society give their services in the schools without salaries of any sort. Many of these teachers are ecclesiastics, many are laymen, and they are often persons of high position. The schools assemble half-an-hour after night-fall, and last an hour and a half. The boys, just as in every Roman school of the better class, are divided off into class-rooms, each with its own curriculum. The course includes the useful subjects of ordinary knowledge; sufficient Latin to read and understand ordinary Latin fairly, caligraphy, elementary mathematics, and linear drawing. Boys who, having exhausted these subjects, wish to continue at school, are put on in more advanced studies, in any line they may themselves prefer. The class-rooms are decorated with specimens of the productions of these boys in caligraphy and design, and even in wood-carving, sculpture, and painting. Towards the close of the year of study they give an exhibition of their works ; they make speeches, defend theses, and are publicly examined in the different phases of the year's study. Princes, Cardinals, and savants come to these exhibitions ; and if any boy shows talent which it is worth while to cultivate, a patron is found for him, and his fortune is made ; so that in Rome, shop-boys, errand-boys, and boys out as apprentices have the opportunity of taking any position in life for which they may be fitted, in spite of the difficulties of the position to which they may have been born.

The boarding-schools for boys, like those for girls, already gone over, are under the direction of Religious bodies. The Brothers of the Christian Schools have a large school in the Palazzo Poli. The Directors are French, and the boys are mostly of French parentage or descent. The terms are about £16 a-year. The Fathers of the Pious Schools keep the Nazarene College, where they receive on an average fifty boys, who are all taught in the College, and are carried up to Rhetoric. French, Drawing, and English are parts of the ordinary studies. The terms are sixty-five francs a month. The boys give exhibitions, when very creditable specimens of caligraphy, drawing, and water-colour painting are exhibited. Many very illustrious Italians have been educated in this College since its foundation in 1602. There are burses for twelve boys in this College. The Sommaschi Fathers have an average of forty pupils at the Clementine College, and the classes are conducted at home, through a course similar to that of the Nazarene College. The fees are sixty francs a month.

The Ghislieri College receives about thirty boys. Most of them are on the foundation, the others pay fifty-five francs a month. The noble College, under the Jesuit Fathers, has accommodation for 100 boys of gentle birth, from any part of the world, and English Catholic nobles have occasionally sent their sons here. The terms are seventy-five francs a month. The boys attend the classes of the Roman College. Outside the city, in the vast Villa Mondragone, near Frascati, the Jesuit Fathers have another boarding-school of the, highest class, recruited from boys of noble birth from all parts of Italy. In this College, gymnastics and physical training generally share the course with the usual subjects of an accomplished education. None of these schools send their pupils home, at any time of the year ; but their parents can freely visit them, and, if they wish, can have them home for short periods. The month of October is spent in villas on the mountains, with a prolonged holiday passed frequently in excursions ; and several of the Colleges have villas or playgrounds, near the city, for other holiday recreations. To this list may be added the schools kept by Monks in their Monasteries—such as the School of the Canons Regular at St. Pietro in Vincoli ; the School of the Benedictines of San Paolo, and two or three others like them. The boys of these schools, according to ancient custom, wear the habit of the Order. They, however, are merry enough when at play in the cloisters, and, according to their own account, pass a happy time of it. The Benedictines have the largest number of boarders.

The means for religious and moral education in the schools already mentioned are very simple. Catechism and Scripture history form the staple of the Saturday afternoon teaching. In the night-schools, the Saturday evening is given up to religious training. On Sunday morning, at eight o'clock, the boys assemble in their various schools, for public worship. Every school has its oratory or chapel ; in every school, but the less important regionary schools, and the parochial and pontifical schools, the whole morning service is conducted in this oratory or chapel, and consists of the singing of Psalms, of a short liturgy, the Mass, Te Deum, and a discourse addressed to the boys by their spiritual Director, which last does not exceed a quarter-of-an-hour. In the public schools there are two or more of these chapels, so as to keep the boys of approximate ages together. At the solemn time of Passion week, the boys of each school have about four days set apart for prayers and special religious instructions, &c., in what is known in the Catholic Church as a Retreat. On Saturdays and Sundays, priests attend for Confessions. Weekly confession is customary with most of the boys, and weekly communion is also very common. Monthly communion is necessary in all the schools, for boys who are of an age to receive Holy Communion. In many of the schools, there is also a Sunday afternoon class, at an early hour of the afternoon.

For physical education, many of the schools and colleges mentioned, even those for the poorest boys, have playgrounds in or out of the city, to which the boys go on their holidays, and on the afternoons of Sundays and feast-days. Day-scholars can, however, go or stay at will. Provision is made in them for the ordinary games of boys. Pallone—a scientific and athletic game of the genus cricket, leap-frog, and prisoners' base, are common games of any Roman playground. The recreation of the boys of the boarding-schools is, however, less demonstrative; a great deal of time is given to walking, and the playgrounds in the colleges are small. In these schools, alone of all in the city, is there any approach to the neglect of physical education, so common in the French and Belgian colleges. Even the very night-school-boys have a fine playground, and every means for hearty sport.

The schools next in order are the Roman Gymnasium of Philosophy, in which logic, mathematics, and physics are taught by four Professors to an average of 100 students,

free of charge. The course extends over two years, and
degrees may be taken in these faculties. The Philosophical
classes at the Minerva, conducted by the Dominican Fathers,
attract from 80 to 110 students. The School of Land-
surveying and Civil Engineering has 70 students, who are
taught by six professors for a fee of 90 francs a-year, in a
course of three years. Successful students are presented publicly with prizes, at an art exhibition given every year. The
Academy School, the expenses of which are wholly borne by
the State, instructs 250 pupils in the Fine Arts, and these also
compete publicly for prizes. The School of Wood-carving,
Architecture, and General Drawing, for young carpenters, is
equally free.

Lastly, and as the culminating glory to such a galaxy of
educational forces, come the Universities and quasi-Universities of Rome. The foremost of these is the University of
Rome, familiarly known, from an inscription on a door-way,
as the Sapienza. This university was founded in 1303, and
has had its days of European celebrity. The Chancellorship
is always filled by the Cardinal Great Chamberlain. The different faculties are presided over by Boards. Of these the
Law Board is the most ancient and most highly privileged;
it has the appointment of the Rector, at the veto of the
Pope, and the Rector appoints his Vice-Rector, at the veto of
the Chancellor. The present rector is the General of the
Servite Order, a man of vast erudition; the Vice-Rector is
a lawyer and a layman. Eight members of the Law Board
are also laymen, the Dean is a layman, and only three of its
members are ecclesiastics. The Theological Board consists,
of course, of ecclesiastics, all men of mark in the various
Orders from which they are chosen. The eighteen members
of the Medical Board are laymen; the Philosophical Board
consists of six laymen and six ecclesiastics; the Philological
Board of seven laymen and five ecclesiastics. The chairs
are won by competitive examination, except in Ethics,
Theology, and Scripture; and these chairs are filled by

members selected from Religious Orders. The number of Chairs, is—

In Theology, six.
  „ In Civil and Canon Law, eight.
  „ In Medicine and Surgery, nineteen.
  „ Philosophy and Mathematics, fourteen.
  „ Philology, seven.

Every subject in each Faculty has its own Professor, with his own lecture-room. Of the fifty-four Professors, only fifteen are ecclesiastics. There are also nine Assistant-Professors, one of whom only is an ecclesiastic. There are nine museums, richly furnished with specimens and materials for illustrating the sciences connected with them.

The schools of the University open early in November and end with July. It is necessary to matriculate by examination, and in order to graduate or compete for honours, one must produce a satisfactory certificate of regular attendance, good conduct, and proficiency, every three months. The lecture-rooms are, however, open to all comers. Matriculated students are examined *vivâ voce* and in writing, at the end of each year ; and prizes and medals are given to those who distinguish themselves. The ordinary course extends over four years, except in the schools of surgery, where only three is required. At the end of two years a student may graduate as Bachelor; at the end of the third year, as Licentiate ; at the end of the fourth year, as Doctor of the Faculty. Those who pass with honours get these degrees free of charge ; those who can plead genuine poverty are also allowed to graduate without cost; in other cases the fees for the Baccalaureat are £2 ; for the Licentiate £2 ; for the Doctorate £8. Notaries, chemists, architects, &c., pay about 25s. for their diploma. The classes meet both morning and afternoon. The school course is entirely free.

The other great University of Rome is the Roman College, erected into a University by its founder, Gregory XIII. In the entire Sapienza, reckoning it by Boards and by Professors, there are only three Jesuits, and these are the great astronomer—Father Secchi, the popular theologian—Father Perone, and the Professor of Arabic and Sanscrit. Neither of these has any place, office, or influence, above that of the other members of his Faculty.

The Roman College, however, is entirely in the hands of the Jesuits, and has been so from the first, except during the short period of the suppression of the Society. Its professors are the pick of that eminent body, the foremost in erudition and in ability to teach of all the teaching bodies of the world. They are thirty in number. The studies include the Faculty of Theology, the Faculty of Philosophy and Mathematics, and the Ancient and Oriental languages. The Roman College is, at the same time, a University and a Public School. Its lower schools take boys from the rudiments of Latin and Greek Grammar, History, Geography, and Arithmetic, up to the most extended reading and composition in Latin, and to a fair reach in Greek literature. Italian literature is also cultivated in its purest modes, and Latin is acquired conversationally, as all the University classes are conducted in Latin. The system is one of remarkable emulation, a perfect model, which nearly all the schools of Rome follow, and which is here in its perfection. In the lower schools, the boys of each school are divided off into hostile camps, which keep up a continued rivalry in study through each month of the year, the victories of each month being posted up monthly in the public corridors. In the higher schools, the system is equally emulative. After the last school of the morning, the students may remain to discuss lecture and to cross-examine each other upon it. Every Saturday there is a public dispute on the matter of the week; every month a dispute on the theses of the month; and at the year's end a long series of tough examinations for places and honours. As in all the boys' schools of Rome, even the poorest, the result of the examination is published at a public prize-giving, attended by Cardinals, Prelates, and savants, as well as by a great gathering of the public, and conducted with all possible ceremony and *éclat.*

The number of scholars of the various grades attending the Roman College averages 1,400. Any boy respectably dressed, and knowing the elementary part of what is usually called education, can be admitted to these schools, and follow them up over the whole range of subjects taught in them. The expense of this education, which, if the modern languages were included, would be the most finished in the world, is merely that of the clothes and keep of the boy while he is receiving it, and of his school materials. The modern languages can, however, be learned from Professors, of whom there are plenty, at a trifling expense; and there are few educated Romans who cannot speak French readily, and many of them learn English. The student can graduate after tough examinations, as Bachelor, as Licentiate, and finally as Doctor in his faculty, without any expense beyond that of the fee for the diploma of the Doctorate, which is about five shillings of our money. No wonder then that these schools number so many externes, and that students from different parts of the world throng to them. Of the pupils in the National Colleges in Rome, those of the French, the German, the English, the Scotch, the Belgian, and the Polish Colleges attend these schools. Here, too, come the pupils of the great Orphan Asylum of Rome; the boys of the Noble, the Ghislieri, and the Pamphily Colleges, with the scholars of the oldest and most venerable of the Roman ecclesiastical Colleges—the Capranica College. And, in yet another point, is this College singularly notable. The Sapienza, indeed, knows no distinctions of rank in those who attend its schools. But at the Roman College, this is more marked, for there are no distinctions even in the lower schools : the sons of princes and of nobles of ancient houses sit by the sons of tailors and of washerwomen, compete with them as equals, and are vanquished or vanquish solely by merit. And this without producing communism or after evil results ; because in Rome, alone of all the Christian world,

has the old Catholic spirit of true brotherhood amongst
classes remained in hearty life.

The first of the quasi-Universities of Rome is the Roman
Seminary, commonly called the Apolinare, from the name
of its church. It averages about 750 scholars. This College
takes rank as the Ecclesiastical Seminary of the Diocese of
Rome, and includes under its roof the Seminary established
by the present Pope for the more promising pupils of the
different Dioceses of the State, each of which can send a
student there. The two Seminaries average about 150; the
rest of the scholars are externes. The classes follow a similar
order and system to those of the Roman College. In the
upper schools are chairs of Greek and Hebrew, of the
different branches of Theology, Law, and Philosophy. The
Roman Seminary is the great seat of the study of Canon
Law, and has special privileges in that study. The scholars
graduate in three degrees, as in the Roman College; and
have disputations and exhibitions, and public prize-givings.
The hours also follow the same order. The Directors and
Professors are secular Priests.

Lastly, there is the Propaganda College, equally a quasi-
University, with a right to confer degrees. There are over
twenty Professors here. The staple of the College consists
of the missionary students sent from all parts of the world
for a liberal education. The studies range over all the
lower and higher subjects of the Roman schools and Universities, including the oriental languages. Modern languages
are taught by the intercourse of the students. The system
is the same with that of the Colleges already described. The
American, Greek, and Irish Colleges send their scholars to
these schools.

It only remains to say that there are many educational
establishments not mentioned in this enumeration, because
they are only indirectly educational establishments. Among
these may be singled out the Orphan Asylum, for boys of
decent birth, generally from seventy to eighty in number,
who attend the schools of the Roman College; the Work-

house of Rome, under the care of Religious, where 250 boys are carefully trained, and their talents developed so successfully that they often turn out men of some mark in the world. And here, I cannot forbear putting before you, my Lords and gentlemen, a point of contrast, worth more than a mere glance in passing. The workhouse boy of England is proverbially a very low specimen of humanity. The workhouse boy of Rome is gentler and more refined in manner than many a noble English boy. And he has much to make him so; he has never learned to look on his fate as a discredit to him; he has kind masters who sympathise with and care for him; he has a large playground, fitted up for gymnastic exercises; round his playground are places stored with favourites of one kind or another—pigeons, rabbits, white mice, or whatever he may fancy; there are little gardens too, which he may cultivate for his pleasure; he may join the brass band of his little community, or practise the pianoforte; and he will have his turn at coming before the world, when, every Christmas and Carnival time, the workhouse boys give plays and musical entertainments in their comfortable theatre. The little articles he turns or carves, his drawings, anything, in fact, he has a mind to distinguish himself by, will be sold to the world, and realise a little sum for him against the day when he has to leave this happy home for the world's work. Nor has a boy in the Industrial School of San Michele less chance than he—and at San Michele, there are 600 orphans of both sexes; and there are many other similar institutions which train poor children to at least a useful life, and not seldom to a life which makes its mark on the little world it moves in.

Another feature of education in the Roman States must not be passed over in silence. The Sunday Schools were in action in the sixteenth century, long before Mr. Raikes began his work in this country. They are in full operation in the different parishes of the State, and very largely frequented. The children assemble in the church in the Sunday after-

noons, having been got together by boys who go round the
streets with a cross and bell, beating up the parish, to the
singing of religious verses. The boys are put on one side of
the church, the girls on the other. They are each divided off
into classes of proficiency, and the teachers are volunteers
from the clergy and from pious lay-people. The elder girls,
when proficient, can try for the posts of teachers, by competition ; and if the duty is well discharged, they are entitled
to dowries and presents from the Society which directs all
the Sunday schools. The male teachers are always volunteers. There is a great deal of emulation in the classes; and,
towards the end of the ordinary scholastic year, the best
boys of the different schools of the city are drafted off to a
special school, directed by members of the Board, where they
undergo a series of examinations and cross-examinations, till
the seven most proficient can stand their ground against the
rest. Then these seven contend amongst themselves, and on
a Sunday in September, the conqueror among the seven—if
he is under fourteen—is publicly proclaimed Emperor of
Christian Learning; four of the others receive the title
of Prince ; the other two are called Captain and Standard
Bearer. The crowning and installation takes place in some
large church, under the presidency of a Cardinal ; and prizes
are given at the same time to other boys, who have distinguished themselves in the various schools during the year.
The prizes of the Emperor and his assistants, are often of
considerable value. After the prize-giving, the Emperor and
his court are taken round the city in the carriages of the
Cardinal-Vicar, under an escort of soldiers. For some nights,
the Emperor holds a levee in his own house ; and during the
few days following his coronation, he and his assistants pay
visits to the Pope, the Cardinals, and the higher nobles of
the city, from whom they receive handsome presents in
money and in kind.. In former days, an Emperor was made
for life, as he could ask the Holy Father for a place in any
public office, for the time when he should be competent to
fill it ; and he was sure of receiving very valuable presents.

For wise reasons this arrangement has been altered; but the money which an Emperor receives in presents secures him a fair start in life, and he can profit, by the public notice he gets, to advance himself when he is old enough. Twice in the year, he assists with his court at public festivals.

And lastly, it must be remembered that the Schools of Rome are not left to themselves. All the Schools and Colleges in the State are under the supervision of an important body, known as the Congregation of Studies, consisting of eleven of the more learned of the Cardinals. It dispenses all the funds for education, and receives and audits the accounts of the disposal of these funds. Reports of the progress of the Schools, and Colleges, and Universities of the State must be frequently sent in to it; and it can interfere in any educational matter which seems to call for interference. The ability and the rank of its members, make this Council the best guarantee for the excellent nature of the education prescribed by the law, and for the manner in which the law is carried out.

To supplement this part of the defence, allow me to mention a fact or two, to show the care for education by which the "liberators" of the Romans have distinguished themselves. There is an ancient University—glorious before the world in the days of our Catholic forefathers—the University of Bologna. In 1865 or in 1866, I forget which, the Chair of History fell vacant. A petition was sent to the Minister of Public Instruction, which was very extensively signed, and which might be said to have been countersigned by the intellect of Italy, praying that Cesarè Cantù, the well-known historian of Italy, might be promoted to the vacant Chair. The Minister declined to agree to the petition, and unfortunately he did more. He appointed to the Chair a friend of his, who had never been known to write a single line on an historical subject, and whose only known literary qualification of any sort was the production of a little volume of comic verses of a very weak description.

The Educational system of the Italian Kingdom was first

introduced into the Kingdom of Sardinia. The other parts of Italy were made to adopt it, as they were in turn absorbed into that Kingdom. Now this system, introduced in 1848, was well in working by the years 1854, 1855, and 1856, in regard, at least, to the elementary schools of the State. In those three years, the official returns of the State, under this head of education, give 327 masters or mistresses "warned" by the Ministry of Public Instruction. Of these, 183 were "warned" for bad conduct. In these three years, twenty-one masters or mistresses were suspended for incapacity, and thirty-one for offences against morals. In the same period, fifty were dismissed for incapacity, and twenty-four for offences against morals. The little Kingdom had, at that date, under five millions of inhabitants, of a race very different to the passionate race of southern Italy. These are some of the educational advantages with which the "liberators" have regaled their own people, since they withdrew public instruction from the care of the Church, and exchanged teachers who educated from a large-hearted charity, for teachers whose chief inducement to teach was the salary to be gained by it.

The next count against the sovereignty of the Pope-King is, that, even if it gives means for a liberal education, it offers no chance of a career to a young man of promise when he has finished his education.

I reply : There is more chance of a career in the State of Rome than in England, and I prove it; first—by the educational statistics already given, which establish incontestably the fact that poverty is not, as in England, a bar to a liberal education, and a liberal education is the ordinary starting point of all careers. I prove it, secondly—by facts. A Roman may easily make a career in the learned and scientific professions, and in commerce. Let us see what chances they offer in the Roman State.

An ecclesiastical career is before any promising student

however poor or friendless he may be at his start in life. The education for this career costs nothing; premiums, exhibitions, benefices, and patrons offer themselves, if one cares to make use of them. If a subject of the Pope-King elects to work in the usual range of priestly life, he has innumerable opportunities for it, in the Hospitals the Night Schools and the Sunday Schools, or in joining in the active work of any one of the various confraternities. The wider field of a parish priest is equally within range, and he can hardly distinguish himself in any one of these walks of life, without obtaining a position in the eyes of his superiors, and so a chance of reaching the high dignities of the Church. The truth, however, is that men who elect this kind of life, are much more likely to desire to remain in it than to wish to be lifted out of it, and the honour of being venerated at the Altar after death is the likelier close of such a career. If, however, an ecclesiastic elects to work in the extensive machinery of the temporal government of the Church—here, again, he meets with no impossibilities, but those of his own making. In the political offices of the State, as we shall presently see, there is a jealous care to give the preference to lay *employés.* But the ecclesiastical offices are open to any one who chooses to try for work in them. The reward of decided ability in them is always, sooner or later, the post of Chamberlain at Court, or selection for one or other of the important Boards of Church or State Government. The Prelatura, the step beyond, is to be gained by competition, as well as by merit; and the two first living statesmen of the Papal States— Cardinals Antonelli and Mertel—rose to it by competitive examination. From the Prelatura, talent and industry may carry a man to the higher ranks of the Episcopate *in partibus,* or to the Cardinalate. There is no better proof of this than the origin of so many of the higher ecclesiastics and Cardinals at this moment in Rome. Cardinal Antonelli, —for example—has attained his high position among the first statesmen of Europe by sheer merit, for he started in life without any family influence to back him.

At this point, one may fairly be met by the objection that this reason is very one-sided, because the State being an Ecclesiastical State, a career in statecraft is possible only to an ecclesiastic. I reply by proving a *non sequitur*. I admit, of course, that the State of Rome is an Ecclesiastical Sovereignty. It would be as incongruous to have an Ecclesiastical State presided over by seculars, as to have a Secular State presided over by ecclesiastics.

The government of a State must follow the nature of the State, as far as the chief direction of the State is concerned. And this is all that is done in Rome. The Cabinet is open to laymen; till lately, two out of the seven members of it were laymen. At present, there is only one layman in the Cabinet; there is nothing to prevent other laymen entering it, but the fact that statecraft is not a favourite study with Italian laymen. Four out of the five Junior Ministers are laymen. In the Department of the Foreign Secretary, eight of the higher *employés* are laymen, two only ecclesiastics. The Secretary of the Council of Ministers is a layman. In the Home Department, the Under-Secretary of State, and the fifteen high officials, are all laymen. The Under-Minister of Commerce, and all the officials, in every branch of the Department, are laymen. So, too, is the Chief Secretary of the Treasury, and so are all the officials of the Treasury. The entire Department of War is in the hands of laymen. In the Senate or Council of State, there is a proportion of ten laymen to two ecclesiastics. The Council of Finance, when the State was in its integrity, consisted of twenty-three laymen and of only four ecclesiastics. The Paymaster-General and his officials are laymen, and so are the Registrar-General and his assistants, and the officials of the Department of Police.

It is false, then, that in public life there is no career before a subject of the Roman States. It is false that the ecclesiastical servants of the State monopolise the places in the public offices. In the lower places there is probably not a single ecclesiastic. And to show that I am not making a wild guess at the truth, I would recommend a careful study of the following figures. In 1856 the Count de Rayneval, French Minister at the Court of Rome, made his report to the French Minister of Foreign Affairs, and he gave a recent proportion of priests to laymen, in the public offices, as follows :—

	Ecclesiastics.	Laymen.
In the Provinces,... ...	15	2,933
In the City	83	2,126

The ecclesiastics in the provinces were the Delegates and Governors of the provinces; "the councils, tribunals, and all the Government offices," he writes, "are filled with laymen." A more recent computation puts the ecclesiastics at 124, the laymen at 6,854. In the number of the ecclesiastics is included the Cardinals in office, and the members of the Diplomatic Body. Add to this number 179 military chaplains and chaplains of prisons, and the return of the number of the ecclesiastics employed in the public duties of the State is 303; the laymen remaining at the same figure of 6,854. The pay received annually by ecclesiastics in office, including ministers and ambassadors, is £224,755, and the pay received by laymen £1,499,747. In the ecclesiastical offices, the salaries of the laymen employed double those of the ecclesiastics. To so great an extent are laymen employed in offices purely ecclesiastical.

It must also be borne in mind that statecraft is not a favourite study of Italians. Even in the so-called regenerated Italy, there has been only one decent statesmen—the Count de Cavour, in the last thirty years. The men who have succeeded him in the affairs of the new Kingdom, have been, almost to a man, professional men without any political education. The present Prime Minister, Signor Lanza, is by profession a medical man. Whereas, in the Roman State, statesmanship is a special science; and men get honours in it, as in other sciences, by the measure of their acquaintance with it. If a man wishes to be a statesman, he has to prepare for it by a course of hard study of law and political

economy. At starting on his career, he is free to pursue it
as an ecclesiastic or as a layman. It is not a question
whether he will be a *priest* or a layman, as is commonly
supposed. By becoming an ecclesiastic, he need only embrace
the lower orders of the state,—need only, strictly] speaking,
receive the tonsure, the mark of the state. He takes no
vows, he sacrifices only the material comforts of a marriage-
state, which he probably has no bent for—for home does not
mean to an Italian what it does to an Englishman—so that
he is free to take the position or reject it, and he can afterwards leave it, if he desires, so long as he has not gained the
superior grades of it, by his own will. In return, he gets the
privilege and place of an ecclesiastic, which, in a city and
State like that of Rome, are both useful and important. If
he elects that place, he has previously set one thing well
against the other. An able man may, of course, become in the
end a Cardinal, and in that case he attains a dignity greater
than the highest dukedom; for he is a prince of a Court
which is not limited to kingdoms and empires, but which
has the whole world for its sway.

This point disposed of, and it is the one which forms the
substance of the grievance, let us see what opportunities a
young lawyer has for rising. If he is an ecclesiastic, he has
the highest posts in the Law Courts open to him; but if he
remains a layman, he cannot aspire so high. The benches
of the Supreme Courts are shut against him; those of the
lower Courts are, however, open to him. There is reason in
this arrangement. The people distrust lay judges in the
higher Courts, and prefer those whose character is more at
stake by an unfair judgment, and who have less to bias them
in their affections and interests. The judges of the lower
Courts, Civil and Criminal, are for the most part all laymen,
as are the judges of the Tribunal of Commerce. A lawyer,
however, has a good position in the country. The barristers
are either barristers who plead, or consulting barristers.
The latter are on the high road to the highest offices open to
them. The barristers who plead are either Advocates of the

Rota, or Consistorial Advocates. These last, like our Queen's Counsels, are an *élite corps*, and possess high privileges; they only plead in ecclesiastical matters, and before the Sovereign. There are also Solicitors, Attorneys, and Notaries, and these last are admitted after examination before the Professors of Law at the University.

In the Medical Profession, the chances of a career are superior to the ordinary run of success in the profession, because of the great yearly influx of foreigners, and of the unhealthiness of the Roman climate at certain seasons. Rome is the centre of the arts; the young artist has a superb career before him in that mother city of art. For men of science too, there is every help to a career; though, in the simpler walks of science, there is a growing tendency to glut the market; and most young Romans one meets, who go in for science, tell you that they mean to be civil engineers or architects. Road-making, bridge-making, and the other works in which the applied sciences come into play are, perhaps, more common in the Papal States than in most other countries; for we shall presently see what a reality the Ministry of Public Works is in the State. Nor is there any impediment to a career when a man aims at the higher walks in science. Rome has produced its share of astronomers, chemists, geologists, and mathematicians. In the present day, the names of Secchi, Antonacci, Volpicelli, Respighi, and the late Calandrelli, are to be found on the lists of most of the scientific academies of Europe.

Nor are the chances of a literary career so poor as they are supposed to be, from the fact that there is a censorship of the press. The object of this censorship is merely to prevent the publication of works against religion and morals. Neither Byron nor Gibbon could have published his works at Rome. It is a question, whether the world has gained as much by the publication of these works as individuals have lost by the reading of them. So long, however, as books are not offensive to religion or morality, their publication is easy enough. And literature in Rome has more

fountains and more channels than people are aware of.
There are the magnificent libraries known as the Vatican,
the Casanatensian, the Angelican, the Alessandrine, the
Barberini, the Corsini, and the Lancisian libraries, which are
store houses of knowledge—all open to the meanest readers,
at fixed hours. There are the ancient and new Academies
—the Arcadian Academy for the cultivation of prose and
poetic studies—the Academy of Archæology, to which all
the noted antiquarians of Rome and the world belong—the
Academy of the Lynxes, for mathematical and physical
sciences, numbering the first philosophers of the world on its
books—the Philharmonic and the Philodramatic Academies
—the Tiberine Academy, for Italian literature—the various
religious and semi-religious academies—and the Academy
of Fine Arts. These hold their sittings, at least, once a month
—many of them once a week ; and any promising young
student is at once sure of an introduction to the world by
their patronage. Rome, too, has its magazines and its news-
papers ; the Civiltà Cattolica can take the first rank in
Italy for its erudition and ability as a Review ; there are
two or three weekly papers, mainly religious and scientific ;
and if the daily papers are small, they contain the telegrams
and a *resumé* of all foreign news. And, after all, when one
thinks how our boasted English press studiously conceals
an unpopular side of things, and represents one view with
all its force, though that view may not be worth the thought
of honest men, one cannot altogether regret that the
papers of Rome are few, and less leaders of opinion
than chroniclers of facts. There is a great passion for publishing just now in Italy, but not a corresponding passion
for thought ; and the productions are as vapid, and, for the
most part, as useless as, in many cases, they are immoral
and blasphemous. The better foreign papers, however, find
little difficulty in circulating. The tables of the cafés teem
with the Debats, and the semi-official Gazetta di Genova,
while more orthodox papers have free circulation everywhere ; and the Siècle, the Times, and Galignani, are to

be met with freely enough in places where people are likely to ask for them. Nor is it true that a strict cordon excludes unlikely books; any book may be obtained for the asking. In the shops frequented by foreigners, books of every hue are on sale. For the cordon is merely meant to exclude doubtful books from a dubious circulation.

Nor in commercial matters, and in matters of general industry, is there any barrier to an honest and profitable career. In the city of Rome itself, commerce is in winter brisk enough; it palls, of course, with the heats of the summer, and the flight of so many residents and visitors. The real question on this point is, however, simply this. Are commerce and industry under such restrictions as to make it impossible or very difficult for them to flourish? The true answer is that they are not. Every State draws a large part of its revenues from customs duties. In States essentially commercial, such as our own country, the lessening of these duties is of far greater importance to the people than in the States only accidentally commercial. Rome is one of these latter. When the Roman State was still entire, the Customs duties of England represented under a third part of the total revenue, while, at the same date, the duties on the Roman State represented more than half the total. But many of the taxes which swell the English revenue are unknown in the States of the Pope; and an increased revenue from Customs duties in that State is not necessarily due to increased burdens, as the following statistics will show. In 1853, the Customs' revenue amounted to £1,048,599. 16s.—in 1858, to £1,566,115. 12s., or nearly a third more. Yet during this period, the imposts had not been increased by a *sou;* the increase of revenue was merely owing to the greater activity of commerce in the State. The duties on salt and tobacco are included in the customs receipts, and not accounted for separately, as in the Budgets of the Italian kingdom. In the Italian Budget for 1867, the duty on salt, tobacco, and gunpowder, was reckoned at the enormous sum of six millions and a quarter,

in addition to over three millions and a half for customs
duties.   Mr. Murray, in his Hand-book for Central Italy for
1850, allows that the customs duties fall lightly on a traveller
entering the Papal Italy.   He might have said that they fall
lightly on every subject of the State; though not so lightly, of
course, as in England, because ours is essentially a commercial country.   It may, however, be useful to compare notes
on one or two articles subject to duty in the two countries,
at a time when we were at peace, and when Englishmen
were as proud of their country as at this moment.   I take
this date, because I can compare the revenues of the
two countries at the time.   In 1843, then, the duty on
foreign sugar in England was 66s. the 112lbs.; in the Papal
States at the same date, 4s. 3d. the 73¾lbs.: the duty on
pepper in England was £2. 18s. 4d. the 112lbs.; in the Papal
States, 6s. 5d. the 73¾lbs.   In 1867, the lowest rate of duty
on our sugars was 8s. the 112lbs., and 11s. 3d. on the purest
kind of unrefined sugar.   The Roman duties have not
increased since the date of the above statistics, so that the
Romans are still more fortunate than Englishmen in this
common article of consumption.   Yet when the sugar duties
were so high in this country, no one thought of arguing that
the commerce in these articles was grievously affected; for
fortunes were made by sugar-dealers and grocers as readily
as they are made now-a-days.   At that date also, the duty
on coffee—as much a beverage of the people as tea is in our
country—was 9s. 9d. the 73¾lbs.   Twenty years later—in
1863, the duty on tea in England was 1s. per lb., and the
coffee duty 3d. in the pound.   In this case, also, the subject
of the Pope-King was the more fortunate.   Cotton, linen,
and woollen goods, iron and hardware generally, formed
the staple of the imports, when the most valuable portion of the State was absorbed into the Kingdom of Piedmont, and on none of these was the duty heavy.

Corn is subject to a special law.   The Roman State, in its
entirety, is made up of lands of very different natural cha-
racteristics, and is subject to great variations from natural
and artificial means.   The great aim of its rulers has been to

give freedom to commerce in these very important matters, with due security to the traders of the State, and a fair gain to the public revenues. In each of the two natural divisions of the State, a weekly tariff is drawn up by the chief representatives of commerce in the division, with tables of the mean market prices of the week. When the mean prices per 640lbs. troy are low, the importation of corn is forbidden, and its exportation is allowed free of duty. When the mean prices are high, its exportation is forbidden, and its importation is allowed free of duty. Between these limits there are two rates, at one of which the importation is subject to a duty of 8s. the 640lbs., and the exportation to half that sum ; at the other, the charges are merely reversed. A similar rule is applied to peas, beans, potatoes, chesnuts, flour, and other cereals, but at a very much lesser rate of duty. In any inquiry of this sort, it must be borne in mind that the native productions of the Papal States are more than sufficient for the needs of the country; that the greater part of the country is fertile to such a degree that there is a second and even a third harvest in some parts of it. So then, if we set down the chief commerce of the State in corn, horses, sheep for wool, wood, charcoal, wool, cheese, alum, paper, silks, velvets, tapestries, hats, wax-candles, and works of art, we give a fair *resumé* of the real commercial features of the State. The alum works near Cervetri have been, in their day, as famous as any in the world. The paper-works of Fabriano supply the markets of many distant nations ; and the annual production was set down at 3,000,000lbs., at its manufactories alone. The tapestries of the State have been fairly sought for in foreign markets. The commercial marine was steadily increasing ; in the years preceding the division of the State, the amount of tonnage and of shipping had nearly doubled. Premiums even were offered for shipbuilding. The zeal of the different sovereigns for the material progress of the country cannot be better evidenced than by their energy in the making of roads, the construction of bridges, and the laying down of water courses. The high

roads of the State are a match for roads in any country; the
noble viaduct of L'Ariccia, the Ponte Mammolo, the new
bridge of Ceprano, are enough to name, to prove the reality
of their work. Gregory XVI. had the reputation of being a
very retrograde Pope; but during the sixteen years of his
reign, steamboats were introduced for commercial purposes
on the Tiber, an arsenal was built at Ancona, the aqueducts
of Umbria were repaired and re-cast, the Anio found a safer
and better course, and the roads were carefully repaired. Who
does not know that, if Rome is the city of waters, if, never
in the long droughts of summer, its fountains are silent, nor
its water-courses empty, it is owing to the care of its rulers.
Only on the very eve of his fall, Pius IX. solemnly opened
one of the grandest monuments of his reign, a new aqueduct
for a quarter of Rome becoming populous, and not so well
supplied as the older quarters. Within our own recollection
two very public streets have been well-paved with raised
foot-ways, a rarity even in the most busy towns of Italy;
and the fine, broad road up the Quirinal has replaced a
narrow lane. Narrow streets are, however, a necessity of
the climate; broad streets would be unbearable in a time of
Roman summer sunshine; and spacious shops with large
windows would be ruinous to their owners, when the sun
fell on them.

Nor would it be just to assert that, under the Pontifical
Government, agriculture has no range for its powers. The
state of the Campagna was a problem in the palmiest days
of old Rome. Cicero tells us that the founders of Rome
chose "a healthy site in a pestilential region." De Re-
publica xi. 6. Livy tells us that the Roman soldiers mu-
tinied, because they had to drill in the pestilential places
near the city, vii. 38. Even the city itself had not a good
name in the summer heats. There was a temple to the
Goddess of Fever in the very heart of it; and Horace, writing
to Macænas from his Sabine Farm, talks of the autumn as a

reason for his staying out of the city, as he wished to keep alive :—

> While the fresh fig and the heats
> Make the undertaker adorn himself, and his gloomy servers ;
> While every father and every doting mother grows pale at the thought of the children ;
> And the dancing attendance on great folks, and the troubles of a lawyer's life
> Bring on fevers, and cause the seals of wills to be broken.
>
> EPIST. i. 7. 5.

It could hardly be expected that a district, even in those populous and powerful times, ill-omened, could be, in our day, one of the healthiest; for the cutting down of innumerable woods, and the other great changes which have come over the surface of Europe, have, as we know, made immense climateric differences felt in the South. The truth, however, is, that in our day there is a hard-working and prosperous population in the mountainous regions of the State; and in the fever-haunted districts, less signs of prosperity, and less opportunity for it. The malaria, be it remembered, is not confined to the Campagna. It haunts the fertile region of the Po near the sea, and the country round Mantua, and some of the most fertile parts of the old Grand Duchy of Tuscany. Over and over again have experiments been made in the endeavour to keep off the malaria; but, hitherto, it has generally baffled for any time the action of scientific men, who are divided about its cause; and even experiments can hardly be said to have fair play with a population which, like all peasant populations, is, in such matters, thriftless. Nevertheless wheat, maize, barley, hemp, and tobacco, are fairly produced in the country, mulberries and other fruit-trees abound in some parts, and vines and olives clothe the hill-sides and the healthier plains. Even Sismondi has spoken with praise of the advanced culture of many parts of the State.

But let us give a glance at the real state of agriculture in that district of the Papal States, which has furnished the text for the hardest language against the Papal Government, on this head of agriculture. The land about Rome is possessed by 113 large proprietors, by the corporation of the great Hospital of the Holy Ghost at Rome, and by the Chapter of St. Peter. It is divided into about 420 farms, each with its portion of arable land, woodlands, and pasture-land. The farms are let to enterprising capitalists, for a fair rent; and they hire their workmen, much as we do in England, from labourers seeking work, who are engaged for shorter or longer periods. The harvest-labourers are in fact just like our reapers, a body of pilgrims in search of wages. Everything in their treatment is regulated by fixed rules, which no farmer can, venture to break. From October to May, over 20,000 labourers are at work on these farms, and the number swells to 30,000 in the harvest time. In some places labour is easy, in others very difficult, where the results are poor from the nature of the land being less volcanic. There are districts in the Campagna which fully repay the labour spent on them, though the plague of malaria withers too often the likeliest plans.

To supplement what has been said on this point, it will be useful to give a few more statistics on the efforts of various Sovereigns of Rome for the promotion of agriculture in the State. In the more abandoned parts of it, Zachary I. founded three agricultural villages; Adrian I. added four to the number; and the figure swelled, under succeeding Popes, to fifty-three. During their stay at Avignon, the Pope-Kings had so promoted agriculture in this distant part of their dominions, that the advanced state of agriculture in the Departments over which their rule extended, is confessedly owing to the fostering care of the Pope-Kings. Gregory XII., by an edict of 1407, promulgated an enlightened system of grain cultivation. Sixtus IV. ordered a third, at least, of every property to be cultivated, under pain of permission, to anyone who chose, to sow it as waste land. The unfriendly Sismondi does not hesitate to defend this edict. Clement VII. introduced free trade, centuries before it was heard of in England. St. Pius V. put an end to the grain monopolies. Sixtus V. founded an agricultural society, by the gift of £45,000 worth of capital, to act as a loan society for persons who cared to cultivate, or to become agriculturalists on a small scale. Clement VIII. took from the feudal laws any clauses which hindered the spread of agriculture. Alex. VII. did away with what restrictions on the trade in corn and cereals remained, or had crept in, up to his day. Pius VI. undertook to drain the Pontine Marshes, and succeeded in making corn-fields of 8,435 acres, and plantations and maize-fields of another 6,386 acres, thus utilising nearly a third of that uncanny district, which had puzzled the rulers of Rome from the earliest ages. By his edict of 1801, Pius VII. announced free trade in corn and cereals, and offered premiums of 3s. 4d. for every four acres and a half cultivated, and a fine of 1s. 8d. for each piece of the same extent left uncultivated. In 1801, he ordered that every town, village, and large farm of the province of Rome, should plant a certain tract of territory, extending a mile one way, with vines, pines, and fruit trees, so that, by degrees, the whole face of the country might become cultivated. He began to found villages, each with its own priest and medical man, to drain marshy places, and to direct water-courses, till the revolution and the French occupation cut short his magnificent designs. In 1819, Pius VIII. offered premiums for eleven years to all who would plant in the Campagna districts olives or mulberries, and this is the result of trees planted, and of premiums given:—

Olives	308,556.
Mulberries	205,703.
Total in trees	514,259.
Premiums paid . . .	£9,256 12s.

A further result was the considerable increase in the silk and oil trade of the country. Under Pius IX., £2,000 a year has been dedicated to rewards for planting trees in the Campagna. In the first six years of this premium, 574,880

trees were planted. Pius IX. has also assisted the commerce
of grain, established a society for the production of hemp,
offered premiums for silk, founded agricultural colleges and
farms, instituted expositions and given medals, introduced
steam machinery and a better class of field machinery free
of duty, and undertaken largely the drying of marshy places,
and the direction of water-courses. In two unhealthy portions of the Campagna, near the city, the present Sovereign
has centred his magnificent efforts to reclaim the Campagna from its present desolation. By founding the Vigna
Pia, with its Reformatory, he has brought to bear upon the
work a class of very useful labourers ; and by inviting the
Trappist Brothers, so remarkable for their agricultural suc-
cesses, to the Tre Fontane, he has raised sanguine hopes of
the ultimate progress of neutralising, in great part, the
present unhealthiness of so large a portion of the district.

    And here I can hardly do better than call your attention
to a feature in the recent history of the Papal States, which
is a triumphant answer to the wild accusations against the
Papal Government, of which one has heard so much. When
the increased opportunities for transport found their way
south, a Company was formed to introduce railways into the
Papal States. This Company consisted mainly of foreigners ;
and it made proposals to the Government, which received
more attention than its most sanguine expectations could
have led it to expect. So far, in fact, from fighting shy of
this new means of intrusion on the privacy and peace of
the State, the Papal Government met the offer with the
most liberal terms of encouragement. The railways of the
State were conceded to the Company for ninety-five years,
A complete highway of railroad was to be made through the
State, to the length of 541½ miles. The property of the
Company was to be exempted from taxation for twenty years;
its public transactions were to be free of stamp and register
duties ; and whatever machinery and material it might introduce for its works was to be free of customs duty, also
for the entire period of the ninety-five years. Especial

facilities were also given for the opening of any branch lines, during the period in which the railways should be the property of the Company. The Government further agreed to guarantee interest at five per cent to all shareholders, by an annual subsidy sufficient for this guarantee. The capital of the Company was £7,000,000 in shares of £6 each; the Treasury made itself responsible for 40,000 shares; the Sovereign also took shares; and, by a Brief to the Catholic world, he recommended investment in these railways, for the advantage of the States of the Church, giving leave to Religious Communities to embark the property of the community in this investment. The State guarantees of the Lombard-Venetian Railway, at this time, only offered to shareholders interest at five per cent., while the Sardinian guarantees realised only four-and-a-half per cent.

This, however, is only one of the many proofs of the readiness with which the Pope-Kings have hailed any effort to ameliorate the material. condition of their subjects. The Anglo-Roman Gas Company was met in a similar liberal spirit. In a similar spirit have efforts to promote the material cleanliness of the city received attention; and the municipal rules of the city could hardly be bettered in this respect. It is but two or three years since a Member of the Lower House—Sir William Fraser—exclaimed, in his place in the House, against the intolerable filth of the London streets in damp weather. The courts and lanes and alleys of London are, however, filthy in all weathers, and there are streets, not very far from great thoroughfares, which are more disreputable than any street in Rome, and with far less of a Christian look about them. And any comparison between the appearance and manners of the people met with in the low quarters of the two cities, would not result to the credit of what is called English civilization. The ragged, unkempt children of the poor quarters of our large cities would, in fact, be looked on by the Roman population as savages in an unheard-of state of barbarism; and the worst quarters of Rome cannot produce anything a hun-

4

dredth part so revolting as the gin-drinking females, who swarm in so many quarters of London. Nor do the Roman streets show anything of that moral filth, which makes our London streets so dangerous to youth after nightfall. The cities of Edinburgh and Glasgow alone, could, however, bear away the palm from Rome, in any rivalry of material filth ; the principal thoroughfares of Rome are clean enough, and the back streets cleanly, in comparison with the less prominent streets of these towns we are so proud of. Every precaution is taken for the collection and the carting away of rubbish. In dry weather, the streets are daily watered and swept at an early hour, after the scavengers' carts have gone their rounds. Because these things escape the eyes of the late-sleeping visitors, they believe that Rome is the city of filth and material neglect. They leave out of consideration, too, the important fact that the streets of Rome are common thoroughfares, not dainty spots like the West-end squares and streets in which our fine gentlemen and ladies pass their days, and that new rubbish must be ever accumulating in them with continual traffic.

The next count is taxation. Is the subject of the Pope King unfairly taxed by a drain upon his gains or his revenues, which can hardly fail to lame his work in life ?

In England, every householder is taxed and rated ; in the Papal States, only proprietors are directly taxed or rated. So that the artisans, the peasants, the artists, and the professional classes as a rule, have no fixed burdens under the Pope-King. It may be objected that, as the taxation must in some way be divided, the landlord must be indemnified by higher rent. The fact, however, is that house-rent is not as high in proportion as in London or Paris; though, with the railroads and the ever-increasing population, the rents have risen considerably in the last few years. But the cause cannot be laid to the taxation, for that has not increased, and rents were wonderfully low a few years back. Nor does the tenant pay by dearness in provisions; the price of bread and meat is regulated in the city by a weekly tariff, and is little above half the ordinary price of these articles in England ; nor are other articles of provision unusually dear. The rise in price of many articles comes, in fact, from the same causes as the rise in house-rents—the increasing population, and the great tide of strangers, which accompanies everywhere the spread of what is, by hackneyed use, termed civilization.

The burden of taxation falls only on proprietors; is that burden excessive ? And here one is obliged to ask leave to bring into court as indirect testimony—the taxation of the Italian Government. For it is the Italian Government which has pleaded the alleged wrongs of the subjects of the Roman State so powerfully, and which has delivered those subjects, at the cost of its own honour and of public justice, from these alleged wrongs. A single instance I have by me, is a fair evidence of the difference between a subject of the Pope-King and a subject of the Italian monarchy, on this question of taxation. A nobleman, one of the foremost nobles of the Papal States, has told me, with his own lips, that a large property of his, which outlies the confines of the small part of the States left till recent events to the Pope-King, pays to the Italian Government in taxation just four times what it paid to the Papal Government, when it formed part of the States of the Pope-King. In this case, at any rate, "liberty" has cost dear.* The only really direct tax of the State is, in fact, the property-tax. The produce of the direct taxes, the year after the cause of the oppressed Romans had been trumpeted to the world by Count Cavour, at the Congress of Paris, was £543,419. 8s. In the same year the direct taxes of the Kingdom of Sardinia brought in £1,067,318. 2s. The population of the latter state was 5,056,000 ; the population of the Roman State was 3,124,178. The excess of taxation was surely on the side of the "liberators." At the very time when the Sardinian Kingdom was proclaiming itself the liberator of the subjects of the

---

* From the same authority, I learn that in two months of the Italian occupation, the taxes on the Romans had increased *three-fold.*

Roman State, the taxation fell heavily on its own subjects, in ways unheard of in the history of the Papal States. A house-tax was producing £160,000 a-year, a tax on patents £120,000, a tax on societies and corporations nearly £40,000, a tax on pensions and public stipends £34,000, an excise duty on unfermented liquors £26,000, a poll-tax £14,000, a carriage-tax £20,500, the register office £480,000, octroi duty £260,760, a stamp duty £248,000; and in the five years, from 1853 to 1858, in which not a single farthing of extra taxes had been laid on the subjects of the Pope-King, the taxes in Piedmont, what with new taxes and the increased rate of the old taxes, had increased by the cipher of £1,258,210. 19s., and this on a population of little over five millions.

The taxation of the Roman State in the year 1857, little more than a year before the political convulsions which dissolved its integrity, brought in the following returns :—

	£	s.	d.
From the Crown Lands . .	70,716	12	0
Direct Taxes	543,419	8	0
Customs Duties and Excise .	853,685	0	0
Stamp and Register Offices .	211,141	4	0
Patents	24,998	16	0
Returns of the Mint . .	3,920	4	0
Miscellaneous Receipts . .	17,650	4	0
Total . . . £1,725,531	8	0

The expenses incidental to this portion of the public revenue amounted to £258,302. 4s. The rest of the revenue was derived from the post-office, the railways, the lottery, and the production of salt and tobacco—the entire revenue that year amounting to £2,563,288. The interest of the National Debt absorbed about two-fifths of the whole. In that year there was a deficit of £90,460. As we shall presently see, by strict economy and increased commercial activity, the deficit yielded, in the following year, to a considerable surplus.

The direct taxes of the State, as we have seen, are taxes on land and other real property. The indirect taxes include a duty on grinding corn and other cereals in mills—a tax which formed a powerful grievance in the hands of the revolutionists, but which has been restored by the Italian Government—duties on salt, maize, and tobacco. There are also communal rates, but these are low, and only made when the communal ·property is not equal to the expenditure. The principal of these are rates on horses and mules kept for purposes of ease, a charge for the passage of flocks, an excise duty on spirits.*

The amount of the Civil List of the Sovereign of Rome is £120,000. The following items of expenditure are borne by the Civil List :—

Salaries of 11 Nuncios, . . .⎫
    „   2 Chargés D'Affaires, . ⎬ Total, £19,380.
Expenses of Embassies and Missions,.⎭
    „   Foreign Office, . .
Salaries to officials in Foreign Office, .
Allowance of Cardinals, . . .   Each, £800.
Expenses of the Apostolic Palaces and
    Chapels, ...
Expenses of the various Ecclesiastical
    Congregations, ...
Salaries of officials of these Congrega-
    tions, when not covered by the fees,
Pay of the Noble Guard, . . .
    „   „ Palatine Guard, . .
    „   „ Swiss Guard, . . .
Expenses of the Museums, Galleries,
    and Libraries of the Papal Palaces,
Expenses of the Court and Household,
    „   „ Royal Table, . .   Average £80.
Repairs of the Façades of St. Peter's,
    and of the Pantheon. . . .

* M. De Rayneval calculates that the taxes in the Papal States are 17*s.* 8*d.* a head, those in France 36*s.* a head. In England, for the year 1866-67 the gross revenue pressed at £2. 6*s.* 4*d.*, and the gross revenues formed the basis of M. De Rayneval's calculation.

Out of the total allowed, a very moderate sum must be
received under each of these items.   The allowances to the
Cardinals and Ambassadors could hardly be found fault with
by the most rigid economist, and the expenses of the Royal
table are too modest to need any apology—they rather in-
vite contrast.*

The debt of the State at the last published return, before the
usurpation of so large a part of it, amounted to £13,500,000.
This would give a pressure of about £4 a head on the population. At the same date the pressure of the debt of France
was a fraction under £8 a head, and that of our own country
about £28 a head.

A brief survey of the financial history of the two coun-
tries which are parties in this suit, will afford further evidence of the injustice of the outcry against the Papal
Government on this point. In the Catholic ages, the Roman
State was rich enough to dispense with taxation. Every
Catholic country thought it a privilege to contribute to the
dignity of a sovereign who was head of the great Christian
Republic, and to the wealth of a State which was the
Mother-State of them all.   With the alienation of so many
countries, the Papal treasury began sensibly to suffer. Immense sums had been expended on the costly buildings,
which thus became the property of the whole Catholic
world.   Direct taxes were introduced by Adrian VI. in
1522, and Clement VII., a few years later, introduced indirect taxation. A few years later still, and Roman funds
were the safest and most popular of European investments.
But the public debt kept increasing; and when Pius VII.
began his reign, it amounted to £11,200,000, while the
revenue was only £600,000.   Pius VI. had already drawn
up a scheme for a just mortgage of a considerable part of the
Church property of the State; the French occupation led,

---

* It is necessary to say that I have reckoned the Roman *scudo* at
5 francs. It generally exceeds it by a sous or two ; but as I have kept
he same calculation all through, it tells equally on both sides of the
question.

however, to the unjust alienation of the whole. But the French occupation, by the application of Church property, and by the necessary check in the temporal machinery of Church government, reduced the debt to £6,600,000. while the revenue, through the increased activity of European commerce, rose to £1,200,000. Pius VII. accepted the previous alienation of Church property, only insisting on the restitution of the Religious Houses, for a fair indemnification to the purchasers.

We may pass over the years which followed the restoration, during which the various Sovereigns were endeavouring, with varied success, to right the finances of the State. For five years after the usurpation of the fairest provinces of the State, the Pontifical Government faithfully paid the interest of the debt of the entire State, which was, of course, a dead loss. The sums so expended were, in . part, repaired by the usurping Government, at the instance of the Government of France; but the past drain was not so easily repaired. It had been found necessary, at times, to increase the public debt; and especially when, at the return of the Papal Government, the Treasury was completely empty, and the country was inundated with paper money, and a copper coinage.* The effect of that revolution, which our liberal Protestants so loudly applauded, was to leave in circulation £172,000 worth of paper money, and £371,498 worth of copper money, gold and silver being almost out of currency. To intensify this state of quasi-bankruptcy, there were new debts with which the State had been burdened, and the commerce and industry of the State had been almost paralysed. In the first year after the return of Pius IX. the Budget showed a deficit of half a million. By strenuous economy, the balance was reduced to £100,000. In 1857, it was only a fraction over £90,000; and in the follow-

* In the partial insurrection of 1831, the municipal treasury of Bologna, alone, was robbed by the Revolutionists, to the extent of over £71,000. The first result of the late invasion was the seizure of the Pope's private funds, valued at over £1,000,000 sterling.

ing year, owing to strict economy, increased commerce, and
the progress of railroads and telegraphs, the deficit had
yielded to a surplus of £28,593. 4s.; and there were prospects
of a still larger surplus, year after year, when the growing
prosperity of the State was so culpably thwarted by the
Piedmontese invasion.

Permit me now to show you the reverse of the shield.
The House of Savoy suffered greatly during the time of French
domination, and at its restoration, it found itself greatly
trammelled with the financial debris of the late state of
things. The debt of the country amounted to a fraction
under £192,219; but for eleven years after the restoration,
it remained stationary. In 1831, it first began sensibly
to increase by a loan of £1,000,000; in 1834, another loan
of £800,000, was contracted; and by new loans in 1841,
and in 1844, the debt rose to £5,400,000, which was still
no excessive burden to a country of nearly five millions
of inhabitants. Then came the liberalistic Governments
of Sardinia, and the public debt became alarmingly on the
increase. The first of these Governments was hardly
born, before it borrowed £2,000,000; in the next three
years, the loans amounted to £14,360,000, and the debt
had reached the cipher of £22,000,000, through new
loans. When, in 1859, the little kingdom began its
aggressions, the debt amounted to £41,800,648 7s. 6d. In
1860, another loan of £6,000,000 was contracted. With the
result of the aggression, the comparatively small debts of
the other States of Italy were added to the large debt of
Sardinia, and an Italian debt was constituted. The debt of
Parma, with a population of 509,000, was £422,329 14s. 4d.;
the debt of Modena, with a population of 600,700,
£442,255 4s.; that of Tuscany, with a population of nearly
two millions, £6,083,200; and the debt of the two Sicilies,
£22,000,000, for a population of nine millions and a half.
In the few weeks which elapsed before the aggression on
Modena and Parma was completed, each of these little States
had been saddled by the Dictator Farini, with a new debt of

£200,000 ; and before the absorption of Tuscany was completed, an extra debt of £2,276,800 was added to its previous cipher. With these burdens, however, came the wealth of all these States and of the Romagna and the other fertile provinces taken from the Papal States—not a fraction of the debt of which had been paid, when, in 1861, a new loan of £28,000,000 was contracted. On the 31st of December, 1866, the total of the Italian debt reached the figure of £211,503,298 10s., and it has gone on increasing, ever since.

The history of the later days of the Sardinian Kingdom, and the history of the Kingdom of Italy, have been, in yet another feature, the direct opposite of the history of the Papal States. To meet the increased expenses, and this ever increasing debt, the country has been loaded with taxation, down to the very minutest object of taxation. It has passed into a proverb, that an Italian has nothing untaxed but the air he breathes. In the years 1853-58, seven new taxes were laid on the Piedmontese, producing, from a country of little over five millions of inhabitants, an additional drain of £392,400 ; while the imposts or taxes already levelled, were increased fourfold, sixfold, and sevenfold. The absorption of territory did not, in the least, diminish the taxation. The new taxes were levelled everywhere at the earliest opportunity, so that literally the rest of Italy was absorbed into the Kingdom of Sardinia ; and the taxation has since been considerably increased. For, in point of fact, there was no other remedy but taxation ; and the alarming deficit year after year, in spite of the prophecies of each successive Minister, necessitated a stern remedy. In the year 1867, for example, that deficit was at the high figure of £12,000,000. Nor had Italy the means at the disposal of the Papal Government. There was little or no political morality in her rulers, and each successive Ministry absorbed all it could. The Civil List of the King is nearly double that of the Sovereign of Great Britain. In none of the Departments has there been any real and lasting attempt at economy ; and members of the Government and officials on Government duty,

have been accustomed to travel at the utmost luxury and
waste, at the public expense. The army is still absurdly
over-officered; and to meet all these burdens, the people have
been ground down with taxation, under the plausible pre-
text that the new state of things being one of transition,
the people must bear the brunt of it. In the Papal States,
on the contrary, economy has been the aim of every successive
Financier of the State, and there has been no temptation to
keep in power by a specious-looking Budget. The Civil
List of the Sovereign is, as we have seen, absurdly small;
and the Papal Treasury could contract loans at par without
difficulty, and could always rely on that handsome yearly
tribute which has kept coming in from all parts of Christ-
endom, since the outburst of revolutionary violence awoke
the deep-seated feeling of the Catholic peoples.

, The next count is that of justice. Are the laws, and the
machinery of the tribunals, such as to promise a subject of
the Pope-King redress of wrongs and a fair trial, if accused
of wrong-doing ?

Trial by jury has not been introduced into the Papal
States; but Prussia has not made use of it, except in the
Rhenish Provinces.* The modern Roman Law is based upon
the old Roman Law, modified by the Canon Law and the
regulations made by different Sovereigns, especially by
Pius VII., Leo XII., and Gregory XVI. In the unbiassed
judgment of M. Guizot, Gregory XVI. dealt most efficiently
with those legal abuses which had crept in with the course
of years, and, especially, through the partial paralysis of the
sovereign authority during the late reigns. The French
Government and the Revolutionists have repeatedly insisted
on the introduction of the Code Napoléon; but the military
precision of the French nature, for which that Code is

---

* Trial by jury has been so much modified, wherever it has been
introduced in foreign countries, as to have neutralised whatever good
it had in it. In a recent number of the "Daily News" this was pointed
out, in reference to the late political trials in Prussia.

Tablet, Oct. 25/79.

PROPERTIES SOLD FOR NON-PAYMENT OF TAXES.

The Government statistics give the following account of properties seized by the fiscal agents of Italy during the last seven years for non-payment of taxes :—

	Ejections.	Taxes due.
Piedmont	73	4,763
Liguria	96	4,081
Lombardy	185	4,407
Venice	198	14,316
Latium (Rome)	205	38,046
Emilia	676	62,360
Marches-Umbria	1,072	81,412
Tuscany	1,083	104,943
Sicily	6,392	528,396
Naples	8,597	620,977
Sardinia	20,077	1,976,816
	39,377	3,440,557

Thus it appears that nearly forty thousand families, previously enjoying a relative independence, being possessed of lands and houses, were driven to desperation by the fiscal exactions of the Italian Government. Assigning five persons to each family, it results that 196,883 persons were deprived of their homes and means of existence. If this had been done undr the dethroned Sovereigns, the so-called tyrants and enemies of progress, what a clamour would have been raised by the Liberal press of Europe! Mr. Gladstone, doubtless, would have written a pamphlet upon State ejections in Italy, and members of Parliament would have denounced in forcible terms the enormity of the cruelties of the petty despots of Italy. But these ejections did not take place under Pius IX., the Duke of Modena, the Duke of Tuscany, or the Duke of Parma. The seizure of estates for non-payment of taxes was rare indeed under the old Sovereigns, whose kingdoms were truly prosperous. Tuscany was then truly called the garden of Italy. Leghorn and Genoa were the rivals in commerce of Marseilles. When earthquakes or inundations afflicted part of Tuscany, the Grand Duke remitted millions of taxes. In 1858, when the Tuscan Government fell, there was a balance of 1,775,000 francs in the Treasury; a balance which was soon changed under the regenerating régime to a deficit of fourteen millions. In the kingdom of the Two Sicilies the public Funds stood at 118, but fell at once to 69 on the rising of the sun of Victor Emmanuel; and 150,000,000 found in the Treasury of Francis II. rapidly disappeared. Sardinia, with 588,000 inhabitants, may be content that only 100,385 persons have been thrown into misery by ejection because they could not pay their taxes. And Naples and Sicily are well off, considering that but 75,000 persons have been turned out of house and lands for the same reason. They have the satisfaction of being ruled by men of their choice, and doubtless bless the day when Garibaldi redeemed them from opulence and happiness to sacrifice themselves for the necessities of the new kingdom.

the Italian
in fact, re-
n adopted,
goes flatly
h the Count
thorities—
tem of the
de, cannot,
l Court to

is simply
20 in value,
lay magis-
ppeal, there
our, or five
ince, which
resumé of
nent given.
dges. From
peal to the
Bologna, and
Rota, dates
cording to a
e Rulers of
and Austria.
ng judges of
omoted to it
re this court
t; and each
a practised
Every cause
arately, and
, before it is
judgment of
most favour-
d Macerata
are equally subject to the Rota, if the parties concerned

have been accu~ waste, at the p over-officered; been ground do text that the n the people mus on the contrary Financier of th keep in powe List of the Sov and the Papal difficulty, and tribute which l endom, since t the deep-seated

. The next cou machinery of tl the Pope-King of wrong-doing Trial by jur States; but Pru Rhenish Provin the old Roman regulations ma Pius VII., Leo judgment of M. with those legal of years, and, es sovereign auth Government anc on the introduct precision of th

* Trial by jury introduced in forei it had in it. In a re out, in reference to the late political trials in Prussia.

and six other Carbonari tried to escape from the Austrians, they were supposed to have been drowned in an attemp cross the Po, or to leave the coast by sea. Nothing was he of him and his companions, and his wife died in 1865 Ariccia, in comfortable circumstances, but in total ignoranc her husband's fate. By her will she left her property, wo some 40,000 francs, in trust for her husband in case he sho have survived. Years afterwards the Garibaldians asser that Brunetti, his son, and six companions, had been captu and shot by the Austrians at Cà Tiepolo on the night of 10th of August, 1849. At all events the bones of eight pers were brought from Cà Tiepolo and placed in a *cape ardente* at the Roman terminus. In the same place were l the bones of men who fell at the Janiculum in 1849, and th of the Italian soldiers killed at the breach of Porta Pia 1870. From the terminus they were carried in procession to Ossario prepared in front of S. Pietro in Montorio, and to 1 demonstration the Italian Government lent its sanction. urn contained the pretended bones of Brunetti and his co panions; four cases contained the bones of the other patri Five ordinary hearses or funeral cars, each drawn by f shabby horses, received the urn and the boxes, the car c taining the urn being equipped like a pagoda or temple. T space in front of the terminus was filled with troops, and so fifty associations, each with an appropriate banner, took part the procession. The most remarkable among these associatic were the Freemasons, whose huge green standard was s rounded, as the *Capitale* boasts, by numbers of Freethinkers, a the association called the Republican Rights of Man Socie whose new banner was still more numerously attended. T Prime Minister, Cairoli, the Minister of War, General Bonel the Minister of Public Instruction, Perez; and the Minister Grace and Justice, Varè, were present at this demonstration especially adapted, is as little consonant with the Italian nature in law as in education. This Code has, in fact, required great modifications wherever it has been adopted, even in France; and in some of its regulations it goes flatly against Catholic rules of action in civil life. Both the Count de Rayneval and M. Guizot—equally impartial authorities— have spoken in very high terms of the legal system of the Papal States; and Englishmen, who have no code, cannot, at least, complain of the objection of the Papal Court to adopt the French Code Napoléon.

The legal system of the State in civil matters is simply this:—All questions involving property up to £20 in value, are taken before Justices of the Peace, and other lay magistrates of the towns and communes. In case of appeal, there is a Court in each province, consisting of three, four, or five judges, according to the importance of the province, which hears both sides, and gives judgment by a formal *resumé* of the case and the reasons for the particular judgment given. This report, and the decision, are signed by the judges. From these Provincial Tribunals, there is a higher appeal to the three great Courts of Appeal, which sit at Rome, Bologna, and Macerata. The Roman Tribunal, known as the Rota, dates from the middle ages, and is partly recruited, according to a very ancient custom, from jurists appointed by the Rulers of the four Catholic nations, France, Italy, Spain, and Austria. These are always ecclesiastics. The eight remaining judges of this Court are natives of the State, and always promoted to it for their high legal character. As the pleading before this court is in Latin, there is no difficulty in this arrangement; and each judge is bound to have an assistant, who must be a practised lawyer of the State, and two legal secretaries. Every cause is put first before each member of the Court separately, and he examines it with the help of his assistants, before it is laid formally before the Court in session. The judgment of M. Guizot, and even of the Italianist Farini, is most favourable to this Court. The Courts of Bologna and Macerata are equally subject to the Rota, if the parties concerned

choose to appeal from them to it. There is also a special
appeal from its own judgment, to a quorum of its most
eminent members. All the Civil Courts of the State, including even the Rota, are, in their turn, put under a High
Supreme Tribunal, consisting of eight ordinary members,
under the presidency of a Cardinal, who has been a lawyer,
with a number of jurists, appointed in successive years as
a consulting body.

For criminal cases, the jurisdiction is equally simple.
Crimes which are punished by small fines, or by short im-
prisonment, are tried before the local Justices of the Peace.
An appeal lies to the Provincial Court, which has jurisdiction over all graver charges. The judges of the provincial
tribunals are free from all interference in their special sphere
of action. The Delegate of the province cannot meddle
with, or undo, the decision of these judges. They have
salaries, and a scale of fees strictly fixed. M. Guizot remarks,
on this head, that the reforms of Gregory XVI. were very
profound.*

From the Provincial Tribunals, an appeal lies to the higher
Courts at Bologna and Macerata. For Rome, and for those
parts specially included under its jurisdiction, an appeal lies,
in all grave questions, to the Sacra Consulta. This last Court
forms the great Tribunal of the State, and alone can try cases
of high treason. It consists of fourteen ecclesiastical judges.
It should also be said that the Provincial Tribunal of Rome
and its district is composed of six lay judges, who are presided over by two prelates.

The process in these Criminal Courts is conducted orally,
and in writing. Lawyers of eminence—all of whom, except
the Advocate-General of the Poor, are laymen—are put at

---

* "A history of our *abortive* attempts to remove admitted defects
in our judicial system, would form an instructive if somewhat melan-
choly volume. For years past the necessity of an *appeal in criminal
cases* has been among the common-places of projected legal reform,
and yet we have, since the year 1844, *five times* unsuccessfully
attempted to carry it into effect by legislation."—*Pall Mall Gazette*,
Jan. 10, 1871.

the disposal of the poor, if they choose to use them. In political charges *only*, is the prisoner *not* brought face to face with the witnesses, though the deposition of the witness is always handed to the prisoner in full. This rule has been found necessary, in the political troubles of Italy, to avoid the party vengeance which would probably fall on the witness. This reason is also of force against the introduction of juries, which, owing to the peculiar nature of the Italian character, would only provoke ill-feelings and lead to unhappy consequences, as so often has resulted from them in political trials in Ireland. The prisoner can call any witness he likes to name, and his counsel speaks last.

Just to show that there is no unusual delay in conducting these trials, it is enough to cite the fact that, in the year before the division of the State, 9,393 criminal cases were disposed of in the Criminal Courts of Rome, of which 3,549 came in the course of the events of that year. Many of these cases were very complicated. The Courts are open to the public, at least, generally ; and the reports of all important criminal cases are published with the judgment and the motives for it, and affixed to the public places of the cities. Civil cases are published in the Official Gazette. The punishments are, in fact, rather too light than too severe ; the punishment of death is rare, and it never follows high treason, unless the criminal has also committed murder. The law against seduction obliges the seducer to give a dowry to the person seduced, or to marry her, or to go to the galleys. Amnesties for political crimes are more frequent in the Papal States than in any other part of Europe. The amnesty of Gregory XVI., in 1831, extended to all but only 38 chiefs of the revolution, and they were allowed quietly to go into exile. Mazzini himself owes his life, and his long series of plots, to the mercy of a Sovereign of Rome. In 1846, every political criminal and exile was amnestied. In 1849, only the members of the Government, of the Assembly, and those officers whose rank in the army was high, were exempted ; and the exemptions were cancelled by degrees, till only 202 Romans remained debarred from the amnesty. In 1859, only 464 individuals—nearly half of whom were in exile—were undergoing punishment for political crimes. Only the assassin of Rossi, and the would-be-assassin of Cardinal Antonelli, were sentenced to death, between 1849 and the separation of the State. John Howard, in his day, found the Papal prisons worthy of praise; so did Mrs. Fry, in her day. The great prisons of San Michele, and the Carceri Nuovi, have been praised by impartial writers for their excellent regulations. Sex, age, position in life, are all considered, and the supervision of the prisoners is not left to paid jailors, but to charitable Guilds and members of Religious Orders, and a Congregation of prelates distinguished for their public character.

You, my Lords and Gentlemen, will remember the strong terms in which, a year or two back, one of the Lower House —Lord Henry Lennox—gave his experience of the state of things in the prisons of the Italian kingdom at Naples. You cannot have forgotten the stern war against the loyalists of Naples in the earlier years of the absorption, or the more recent bombardment of Palermo. You, as English legislators, think it right that rebel Fenians should be punished—can you deny to the Government of the Papal States the right to exercise similar judgment? The more liberal Italian papers, and the Deputies of the Italian government, have, in turn, complained of the barbarous tortures inflicted on prisoners in the prisons of the Italian Kingdom at Parma and at Naples; and our own prisons have occasionally cruel tales to tell. But no such charges could be brought against the Roman prisons, because they are under the surveillance of men who work from pure charity to their kind. And, even if a Roman may occasionally be the victim of calumny, has not such a thing happened here before now? Have not many persons seized for Fenians been proved guiltless? Is it possible to forget the numbers of fathers of families, and only sons of parents, who have been dragged off to prison and the galleys, and who are left to

wear out life there, in the kingdom of Naples, under its new
rulers ?

About one class, however, of Italian criminals—the brigands,
the English public is particularly sensitive, entirely forget-
ting that the roads of England, so long as they were the
chief means of communication, were always more or less
infested by daring and audacious highwaymen, and that
equally daring highway robberies have been committed in
the south of France, within a very few years.   Highway
robberies, in the form of street attacks, are still common
enough in our own city streets; and only four years ago, a
lady, standing at the corner of Sloane Street in London, at
four o'clock in the afternoon, was attacked in that very public
place, and robbed effectually, in the midst of a crowd of
passers-by.   Such robberies in Rome are very rare, and are
always made much of when they occur.   House-breaking is
rarer still.   In our country, both are unfortunately so common
that we have ceased to think much about them.   In Rome,
they are still more than a nine days' wonder.   And with
the employment of peasant troops against brigandage, that
plague has wholly ceased in the Pope's dominions, while it
flourishes as it never did before in the South of Italy and in
Sicily, and has its ramifications in the central and northern
parts of the peninsula.   For the true germs of brigandage
are excessive taxation, stern military conscription, and
general political immorality.*

To supplement what I have said on this point, allow me
to bring forward the following statistics.   The entire number
of prisoners, tried and waiting trial, in the Pontifical States
in 1858, a year before the usurpation of the provinces, was
10,283, including prisoners of every shade.   In the twenty
months, from May, 1854, to December, 1855, the number of
cases brought up before the tribunals of Piedmont was

---

* In August, 1863, eleven of the sixteen provinces of the Kingdom
of Naples were declared in a state of brigandage by the Italian authorities, and as such ruled by martial law. See " Memorie de nostri
Tempi," vol. iii.

11,534. Of these, 7,794 were for thefts, 204 for homicide,
1,893 for cutting and wounding ; 1,105 for highway robberies. The cipher of prisoners—tried and waiting trial—
in the Papal States was, in the same month of December,
1855, 11,656. It may also help to a fair judgment on this
head, to bear in mind that during the year ending September 29, 1866, 481,770 persons were brought before the
local magistrates in England and Wales, of whom 339,091
were convicted. During the same year 27,190 other persons
were charged with more serious offences, of whom 18,449
were committed for trial. In the same year, the offences
under the head of larceny, were 18,725. Equally may it
with profit be recollected that, by the statistics of 1864,
there were then, in England and Wales, 21,734 houses of ill
fame, and that the criminals *at large* were reckoned at
116,749. The population of England and Wales was at this
date 20,066,224, or only six times that of the Papal States.

I may also be permitted to give these other statistics of
the Italian kingdom. The number of conscripts in three
years, up to the 30th September, 1863, who had run away
from the conscriptions, many of them to swell the ranks of
real or so-called brigands from sheer necessity, was 59,386,
nearly half of whom were in the prime of life. Up to April,
1863, in less than three years of its occupation, the merciful
Government of the Italian kingdom *shot* 7,151 persons in the
Kingdom of Naples, many of them in cold blood. At the
same date, there were in the Neapolitan prisons 4,040 persons charged with political offences. Now it must be remembered, that the Neapolitan kingdom had been invaded
by force of arms, and that the votes for its annexation to
Italy were ridiculously few. Numbers of Neapolitans pre-
ferred their autonomy and the rule of the Bourbons, to the
new regime of fire, sword and taxation. With all such persons,
the Government was merciless. It christened them with the
name of brigands, to turn the pity of Europe from them, and
then murdered and imprisoned them. In the prisons of
Sta. Maria Apparente at Naples, on the 22nd January, 1863,

were the following prisoners—still untried or still uncondemned :—

Number of Prisoners.	Time in Prison.	Remarks.
1	2 years.	Without trial.
1	21 months.	Without trial ; put to hard labour.
4	20 „	Without trial ; 2 put to hard labour.
6 .	19 „	Without trial ; 4 to hard labour—2 without sentence.
22	18 „	All without trial ; 2 in chains—1 solitary confinement—13 hard labour.
7	17 „	All without trial ; 5 to hard labour.
2	16 „	Without trial ; 1 to hard labour.
2	15 „	Without trial ; 1 to hard labour.
1	12 „	Without trial.
1	11 „	Without trial ; flogged.
2	10 „	Without trial ; 1 to hard labour.
1	9 „	Without trial.
4	7 „	Without trial ; all to hard labour. *

The kind of justice with which the Italian Government benefits the people it "liberates," needs no comment after these simple facts.

Thus, step by step, we have carried our inquiry up to the last and most important point of the whole machinery of government in the Papal States. For a good system of government would neutràlize, in time, any evils which might exist in any department of the public service, any defects in the ways and means of public life. But if these were only in theory ever so perfect, they would be very effectually neutralised in practice by a system of government rotten at the core. Permit me, then, to defend that much accused system of government which directs the fate of the Papal States, by a simple statement of its true nature.

* The names of these unhappy people, whom Mr. Gladstone passed over in silence, are all published to the world, at Turin, 19th February, 1863.

The absolutism of the Pope-King consists more in name than in reality. He directs the State rather as the supreme fountain of power, than by his own judgment. He decides nothing without taking the advice of his counsellors—statesmen reared to their work. He has a Cabinet, consisting of six Ministers and a statesman without a portfolio. The number of Ministers is not necessarily limited, if the needs of any branch of the administration seem to require a greater division of the public service. When the Pope-King had a larger territory, he had, at one time, as many as nine Ministers. His rule is to receive his Ministers at least once a week, on fixed days and at fixed hours. The more important members of the Cabinet are, however, received twice a week ; and the Premier, three times in the week. A Cabinet Council is held every week, and its decisions are voted by majority, then submitted to the Sovereign, if he has not himself presided at it.

The Ministers who compose the Cabinet are the Foreign Secretary, who, as in Prussia and in Austria, is also Prime Minister, the Home Secretary, the Secretary at War, the Minister of Finance, the Minister of Public Works and Commerce, and the Director General of Police or Minister of Justice. It will be well to look into the duties of each of these ministers more in detail.

1. The Foreign Secretary, as Prime Minister, has important functions at home, and is the great link of communication between the State and its Sovereign, in all those matters which affects its vitality. In this, he occupies a position more real than an English Prime Minister, but hardly more so than the Premier occupies in Prussia or in France. He has an Under-Secretary, and a staff of clerks and assistant secretaries.

2. The Home Secretary has duties similar to those of our own Home Secretary, including the general supervision and arrangement of the Law Courts and Tribunals, of provincial and municipal government. He too has his Under-Secretary, appointed by the Crown, his staff of secretaries and officials.

Under his control are the following Departments of the public service—

The Council of the Roman Province,

The Public Record Office,

The Board of Health,

The Direction of the Prisons,

The Direction of Police,

The Local Police,

The Presidencies of the various regions or quarters of the city,

The various Law Courts and Tribunals of the State.

3. The Secretary at War has merely the usual duties of his particular office. He has an Under-Secretary, and is assisted by a Council, and by the heads of the various Departments.

4. The Minister of Finance has the direction of all the finances of the State, and prepares a Budget, which is afterwards approved or amended by the great Financial Board which will be alluded to presently. He is assisted by and regulates the following Departments—

The Council of the Treasury,

The Commission for the Liquidation of the Old Public Debt.

The Direction of the Public Debt, in its several departments,

The Direction of the Taxes,

The Board of Customs and Excise,

The Stamp and Registry Office,

The Salt and Tobacco Office,

The Direction of the Posts of the State,

The Direction of the Mint,

The Direction of the Lottery,

The Commission of the Land-tax.

5. The Minister of Public Works is also Minister of Commerce, Fine Arts, and Agriculture. His office is divided into Departments, besides which, he is assisted by the following independent Committees or Boards—

5—2

The Commission of Fine Arts,
The Commission of Antiquities,
The Commission of Roads, Water Works, and Public
    Buildings,
The Direction of the Telegraph,
The First Chamber of Commerce,
The Chambers of Agriculture, Commerce, and Industry.

6. The Director General of Police, who has the rank of
Minister, is assisted by an Under-Secretary and several
higher officials. His office is divided into the following Departments—

Political Censorship of the Press,
Pure Police,
The Lesser Tribunals,
Passports,
Personel of the Force.

There is no Parliament, nor is there nominally a Senate.
Parliaments have not worked well in Italy; there are many
who think that Parliaments are only suited to the race
which gave them birth. However that may be, one must
not suppose that the Ministers of the Pope-King have it all
their own way with the Sovereign and the people. There
exist certain strong and useful checks on the Ministers, in
the Council of State—which answers to a small Senate, and
in the Council of Finance. The Council of State—an
institution, by the way, equally existing in Prussia and in
France—consists of a President, Vice-President, Secretary,
and twelve ordinary members. Any Minister can attend
its meetings, but he has no vote in its decisions. It is
divided into Standing Committees. For legal difficulties
in the administration, there are three Committees: the first
hears the case; the second takes it up on appeal; the third
revises the final judgment. The decisions of the Council on
these questions are final; the Sovereign merely counter-
signs them. For questions of government and mere administration, there are two Committees. The decision on

these questions is not final: the report is sent in to the Sovereign, who decides, after hearing from the Minister concerned, his side of the question. The Committees sit twice a week. Any question of unusual importance is laid before the whole Council, which meets once a week to revise the matters which come before it and for general discussion. All kinds of matters come under its cognisance. It examines proposed laws, or proposed new interpretation of laws, and discusses as well provincial and commercial as ministerial questions. At one time this Council was an elective body ; by the present rule Senators are nominated by the Sovereign, just as the House of Lords, or. a Senate in other countries, is nominated.

Another check on the Ministry is the Council of Finance, which bears to the Treasury much the same relation which the Court of Exchequer is supposed to bear to the Treasury of Great Britain. It consists of twenty members. Four names are sent in by each Provincial Council, selected by that Council from the proprietors and wealthier commercial men of the province, and from the Professors of the University of the province, if there be one. The Sovereign selects one, as the Queen pricks for sheriffs. Five other members are added to the Council on the nomination of the Sovereign, to represent the property of the Crown. Every two years, a third part of the members of the Council retire from office, to make way for new blood. The Council sits for three months in each year, and during that period, its members assemble three times a week. It deliberates on all questions of the national debt, on the making or abolishing of taxes, tariffs, and commercial treaties. Every six years it compares the past Budgets with one another, and with the actual expenditure, and prepares a general Budget for the next six years. Every year it revises this scheme, and prepares for the extraordinary expenses likely to be incurred in the course of the coming year. It has power to deal with the minutest particulars of the public expenses. Several times in the last few years, the Budget prepared by the Finance

Minister, has been revised by the Council, before it has
adopted it, and the amendments of the Council have been
sanctioned by the Sovereign. These amendments have
always been on the side of greater public economy.

Another less important council, but in its way equally
useful and independent, is the little Council of Financiers
which occupies itself with the adjustment and re-adjustment
of the tax on real property. It is formed of the more states-
manlike among the Cardinals, the Home Secretary and the two
more important Financiers of the Treasury, with the Minister
of Finance, and any other Financier or Financiers of eminence,
whom the Sovereign may nominate. When the State was
in its entirety, this Council held an important place in the
Government; it was a sort of registry office for a large
extent of territory. In its less extended capacity, it still
performs good service as an appeal from the worries of small
tax-collectors, and other communal officers. It has its staff
of civil engineers, who inspect and make returns, with a
number of special revisers, and, lastly, a Committee of Re-
vision — the revising body consisting entirely of civil
engineers. It is hard to see what better security against
over-taxation could well be had; and the strict justice and
care of its returns have been repeatedly praised by economists
who have investigated them, or examined the principles upon
which the adjustment of this important tax proceeds.

Nor are the interests of the commercial classes left
entirely to the Minister of Commerce. The First Chamber
of Commerce—a liberal kind of Board of Trade—exercises an important influence on the commerce of the
State, and looks after the interests of the commercial
classes. It is composed of fifteen members, a third part
of whom retire every year, when the remainder send in
the names of fifteen candidates to the Minister, who nominates five from the lists. The President remains in office
three years, and one of three names sent in to the Council of
Ministers is selected when he retires. The Chamber elects
its own Vice-President, and meets every fortnight for or-

dinary business. It has a Secretary, an Accountant, and
a Keeper of the Records. It has also the right of electing
the judges of the Tribunal of Commerce; for which it pro-
poses a list of ten names to the Minister. He selects two, and
names a distinguished lawyer for the legal business, and two
others especially to decide on matters involving special knowledge of commerce, and these last are renewed every two
years. The members of this Chamber are exclusively
laymen.

There is also an Exchange at Rome, presided over by one
of the members of the Chamber elected by itself; and a body
of licensed Stock-brokers. And to assist the Minister in the
important departments of Agriculture, Commerce, and General
industry, there are special Boards, consisting of persons eminent for their knowledge in the matter of each Department.
In that of Agriculture there are seven members, with the
President and Vice-President of the Chamber of Commerce.
These also form part of the Board of Commerce, formed of
five other members. The Board of Industry has six members.
All these, again, are laymen.

The State is divided into Provinces. There are twenty in
all; and each province is presided over by a President
who resides in the chief town of the province. In the four
more important provinces of the State the President is a Cardinal Legate, who, as representative of the Sovereign, keeps
a little court in the chief town. In the other provinces, the
Presidents are called Delegates, and have less extended
powers. They are generally ecclesiastics and lawyers of
eminence. In fact, the Delegations are schools of government, through which every aspiring statesman has to pass.
There are occasionally lay Delegates, when the opportunity
to test the governing powers of a layman of mark has oc-
curred. Lay Delegates have not, however, been popular.
Their surroundings of property and of family connection
have made the people suspicious of them; and in one case—
that of Ferrara—during the present reign, it became necessary to replace a good Delegate on account of this oppo-
sition.

The Legations and Delegations are again sub-divided into Governments. When in its entirety, the State has 177 governments. The real administration of the province is, however, in the hands of a Provincial Council. To be eligible for this Council, one must be a proprietor in the province, with property worth £1200, or a tradesman, whose property is valued at £200, or a professional man or artisan, with £100 worth of property, real or personal. The election rests with the communes of the province; but out of the three names chosen, the Sovereign selects one. The Council meets twice a-year in the chief town, and its sittings last three weeks. Two-thirds of the Councillors must be present, to pass any measure; the voting is by ballot. For the ordinary business of the province, the Council nominates a Standing Committee of three members.

The Legate, or Delegate, is also assisted by a Governing Council, composed of five Councillors named by the Sovereign. Two of these are taken from the members of the Provincial Council. In questions of finance and revenue, the decision of this Council is final; in other matters merely consultive.

The Governments again are sub-divided into communes and towns. At different times, different Sovereigns have conferred charters on the communes and towns, which have guaranteed their liberties, and consolidated a system of Municipal government. Each town, each commune, has its own Council. The commune of 1000 souls is represented by 18 Councillors. That of 1000—3000 by 24. The towns of lesser importance have 36 representatives; the larger towns, 48. The people elect these Councillors; the condition in the candidate is, however, respectability and intelligence. Two-thirds of those who are eligible must be proprietors; the remaining third is taken from those inhabitants who, pay a fair share of rates to the commune. Only day-labourers, and the lowest class of townspeople, are ineligible for the Council; and, in fact, every decent class, but one, gets more or less represented in it. The clergy, alone of the respectable inhabitants of the commune, are ineligible for Councillors; but two members of the same family cannot be elected to the same Council. Unless half the voters of the commune are present at an election, the candidates returned are not duly elected. When the Council is constituted, it elects its own officers; a majority of two-thirds present being required for each officer elected. In the present troubled state of Italian politics, it has been considered prudent to put a restriction to this rule, so far as it applies to the Mayor and Aldermen of each commune. For the election of each of these, three names are chosen by the Council, and forwarded to the President of the province, who selects one in each list.

The smaller communes have only two Aldermen—literally elders; the larger have six. The appointment is only for two years; half the number of Aldermen, and the Mayor, then retire, but they may be re-elected. They receive no salary for their official duties, and no payment, but some very trifling fees, to which they are entitled for certain occasional extra duties. The Mayor need not be a member of the Council, either before or after his election; but he has to administer the regulations made by it. The Aldermen, on the other hand, must be members of the Council, to be validly elected.

The Council has, however, certain checks on its freedom, which it is only fair to mention. In the smaller communes, the existence of these checks is a great safe-guard where there is not a manhood suffrage. Without them, these communes would have a liberty rare enough in our days; for the law *obliges* the superior authorities of the provinces to recognise the Council when once elected. The Council cannot part with communal property, or borrow for communal purposes, without the consent of the Government coming through the Delegate. The making of new rates, the little budget of the commune, and the precis of the deliberations of each meeting of the Council must be submitted to the Delegate of the province. These checks are of great use in the

present day, when the volcanic state of Italian politics has
so ma terially injured the property of the communes, as to
make it more than advisable that the funds of the commune
should have some supervision, outside of communal interests.
The general business of the Council is to look after the property of the commune, and especially its roads and water-
courses; to make its yearly Budget, reducing as much as
possible the rates and dues, and to see to the public health
of the commune.

The government of the city of Rome differs, however, in
some sort, from the system already described. The city is
divided into fourteen wards—rioni or regions—each presided
over by a magistrate. This magistrate has the rank of Major,
in the precedence of Roman society. To assist him, he has
another magistrate, with the precedence of a Captain in the
army, and a secretary. He has at his disposal a little force
of gendarmes; and his business is to keep a general register of
all the inhabitants in his ward, carefully noting the changes
of population every month. He has to send to the Minister
of Police a daily report of the state of the ward entrusted
to him. These magistrates are selected by the Minister of
the Interior.

The real administration of the city is, however, in the
hands of a Town Council, elected by the citizens, from among
the different classes of citizens whose character and position
entitle them to the office. These, again, elect eight Conservators, answering to the aldermen of an English corporate
town, if not in the manner of election, at least, in the nature
of their office. Twenty-four names are sent to the Sovereign,
who selects from the list the persons who seem fittest to
represent the interests of the city. The election is for six
years; half the number retiring in the course of that time.
The Chief Magistrate is the Senator, nominated by the Sovereign, from one of the noble families, for six years. The
present Senator—the Marchese Francesco Cavaletti—has
discharged his office with great ability, and has done much
for the material improvement of the city. The Senator re-

ceives no salary ; his office is, however, no sinecure. He has to discharge the duties of Chief Magistrate, and to look after the general welfare of the city. He is assisted by the Conservators, and by a Secretary-General with two assistants. The affairs of the city are more immediately managed by the Departments of his office, each of which is sub-divided into Committees for the direct supervision of each branch of the municipal service. It is almost needless to say that these matters are entirely in the hands of the lay citizens. The Senator, in return for his services, has special rank at court, and certain privileges of office ; but these are not enough to attract a man to the office, which is, therefore, one of real public duty.

The subject has grown upon me. I might, indeed, have gone still more minutely into many details, without exhausting the subject. The deeper one goes into it, the more sterling ore one finds. But I have said enough to convince you, my Lords and Gentlemen, that the popular idea of the rule of the Pope-King, and of the state of his subjects, is totally false. Its basis is, in fact, the readiness to believe anything ill of a foreign government—there is the national and insular prejudice ; and the disposition to accept anything that can be said against the temporal rule of the Pontiff of a religion detested by one's dearest instincts—and this is the religious prejudice. Protestant statistical writers have approached the subject of the Papal States, with the strangest. prejudice and ill-will to find anything good. They have drawn their information from persons utterly untrustworthy, because rabid with political animosity to the Government. They have set down everything as irretrievably bad; and have shut their eyes to the labours of Sovereign after Sovereign to ameliorate, to redress, and to elevate, the state of the people under them. The Motu Proprios, or Bills, of each Sovereign are to be read ; they have never read them. Even Mr. Macculloch—a man so distinguished in statistical knowledge—can find nothing but abuse for the Papal States,

and forgets all his usual rules for seeking knowledge, when
he comes to treat of this defenceless little State.

A curious instance of the way in which people bring
charges against the Papal Government is to be found in the
writings of two men, who have done much—the one in Ger-
many, the other in England and America—to embitter people
against the rule of the Pope-Kings. Mr. Story—in his Roba
di Roma—tells us, that " in Rome all the masters are priests."
Yet Mr. Story had lived in Rome for many years, when he
wrote that book ; and he says, in this sentence, not only what
is directly untrue, but what is the more shamefully untrue,
in that the great majority of schoolmasters and professors in
Rome are not priests, or ecclesiastics at all. Dr. Otto Förster
—in his " Italy and its Political Situation," published at
Leipsic, in 1859,—says of the agriculture of the Papal States :
" The government of priests has always neglected the interests of agriculture." Compare this assertion, I pray you,
with the statistics on this very point, given in the previous
pages of this pamphlet, and then say what sort of faith can
be put in a writer, who so flatly contradicts plain and established facts.

But, you will say, there must be a reason for this hatred
of Papal rule—whence does it come ? It comes, my Lords
and Gentlemen, from sheer hatred of the Christian religion.
The fruits of the principles of the French Revolution, which
survived the French domination in Italy, were hatred of
Christianity and hatred of authority of every kind. The
Secret Societies, leagued against both, swarmed over Italy,
swarm over it still. To them all government, but the
supremacy of the individual, is hateful ; and that religion
which inculcates moral order is, therefore, to them supremely
hateful. This hatred has been intensified from a strange
cause. The Pope-Kings have dealt very leniently with
merely political criminals—with men, who, if Fenians, must
have been early sent to the scaffold, by our severer rule—
and this clemency has intensified the hate. The Italian nature
is proud, hates to be under obligations ; and to owe life and

even liberty to a Sovereign, who was also a priest of a detested religion, has created a sense of obligation positively galling. If Signor Mazzini had not owed his life and his liberty to the clemency of Pope Gregory XVI., when he merited death for his political plots, he would never have hated the Papal rule half so bitterly. Then, it is true that the plain rules of Christian life, taught by the Catholic Church, and made superior to other considerations in countries where it has authority, are very trying to those subjects of the Pope-King, who cannot bear to lead the lives of ordinary Christian men. On those young men, whose bent has been for evil, this yoke has pressed heavily. But of the great mass of the people, this is not true ; they are happy and content enough ; their evils are nothing like so heavy as those the English artisan so often cries out against ; they have perfect liberty to grumble if anything worries them ; in fact, nothing, perhaps, strikes the thoughtful foreigner more than this same large liberty of giving utterance unchecked to any cause for complaint, real or imaginary. Under the Italian rule, men speak with bated breath—they are very open-mouthed under the Roman rule.

And, lastly—if it should be urged that the theory of government is good, but that its practice may modify the judgment of any thoughtful man—I reply. I do not argue that in all points theory is borne out by practice—this takes place nowhere on this miserable earth ; as well with the worst as with the best, the rule holds good. And, surely, our English Constitution, which is so perfect in theory, breaks down in practice, in many points, as utterly as does that famous Constitution which, having for preamble that all men are born free and equal, yet allows of that bitter race hatred between the white man and the coloured man, which is such a curse of America. But I do maintain that there is as fair play in the Papal States for its excellent Constitution, as there would be for it in any other country—and I might easily attempt to prove that there are even fewer gaps between the theory and practice of go-

vernment in the Papal States than in other countries. For I
assert that the peculiarity of the Sovereignty is the great
security for the good working of the Constitution; and I think
that the working of each part of it by men trained and
qualified to apply it, is a rare fortune for its subjects.

The Italian rule has, at least, brought no advantage or
promise of advantage. Three years ago, the liberal papers of
Italy published statistics and letters to show that the trade
of Leghorn and Naples had utterly collapsed, since the
absorption of those towns into the kingdom. The public
debt grows; taxation increases; there 'is' never a stable
ministry; the expenditure is ruinous. Emigration—a thing
unheard of in Italy before—is now the resource of thousands
yearly. Italy, the fertile and the beautiful, of whom it was
said a few years ago that none of her children could die of
starvation, now witnesses that sad close of life, often in the
course of the year. The picture of the Italian Kingdom, as.
represented in the liberal papers of the country, is enough
to sicken its fondest supporter. No one stands by it, but
those who make their bread by the Monarchy. Great
apathy and a sense of despair have fallen on the people—very
few go to the urns to elect deputies or communal officers.
For they know that all alike are venal, that the great aim of
successive Ministers and officials is to grow rich. And only
the other day, when Rome was suffering from the absence of
foreign visitors, and the stagnation of trade consequent on a
great political convulsion in the country, the new authorities of Rome decreed that £12,000 should be spent on the
decorations for the reception of King Victor Emmanuel.

And any one, who remembers those mighty outbursts of
popular devotion, when the people of each region would club
together to make the city glorious for the anniversary of the
return of the Pope-King from Gaeta; or, again, who wit-
nessed the reception of the Sovereign, when he went to
the Church of the Santi Apostoli, the day after the French
left Rome in 1866—a reception which made Mr. Gladstone
wonder-struck; or, who was present when the victorious

army of Mentana entered the city, amid the shouts of the
people ; or, again, who beheld that mighty gathering, and
heard its voice on the 10th of September, ten days only before
the city was to fall to a secular rule, when the Pope-King
went to open that splendid monument of his reign—the
bringing in of a new water-supply to a quarter of the city
where it was scarce—he, I say, who was privileged to behold
any of these things, can have only contempt for the late
Plebiscitum. The liberal world uses plebiscita, and laughs at
them ; the returns of all the Italian Plebiscita are before us ;
their total is little more than that of a tithe of the people.
And the late Plebiscitum of the Roman States took place
only when the bayonets of the invader surrounded the urns ;
it was conducted without any security for age, or nationality,
or citizenship, and in plain violation of all the regulations
which had been trumpeted forth as guarantees for this security; and it came off when the city was flooded with people
from all parts of the Kingdom, the greater number of whom
were professedly sent to vote at the cost of the public.

And, indeed, I know not with what face any honest man
can take his stand on the Plebiscitum, as an argument
against the Temporal Sovereignty of the Popes, after the
following paragraph, which appeared in a Roman newspaper
a few weeks since.

" A distinguished mathematician of our city, has compared
the number of votes said to have been given in Rome, on the
2nd of October, with the length of time the voting lasted, and
the number of urns placed to receive the votes, and so made
a calculation as to how many persons a minute could have
given their votes, to produce the total return. The *Si* were
returned as 40,785 ; the *No* at 46—total 40,831. The voting
lasted 10 hours—from 8 A.M. to 6 P.M. There were 12 urns
in all. So at least the official Gazette informs us. 10 hours =
600 minutes × 12 urns = 7,200 ; 40,821 ÷ 7,200, gives 5.67
votes per minute. To get the published result, it was therefore
necessary that the voting should have gone on during the
whole 10 hours, at the uninterrupted rate of $5\frac{1}{2}$ voters a minute

for each urn. This seems impossible on the face of it; but its
impossibility is clear, when we consider how the voting pro-
ceeded. The voters had to mount up steps to the polling-
booths, to present a ticket of admission, and, in most cases,
had to select there and then, the *Si* or the *No* presented for
choice. Now it is a fact, that, for the first two hours, the
voters presented themselves very sparely, and at intervals,
for direction had been given to vote as much as possible in
trade companies. Eye-witnesses affirm that during the
afternoon hours, the booths remained almost deserted. A
person has himself assured us, that he remained watching
the booths on the Piazza Navona [a most public square, in
the heart of the city] for more than an hour, and during
that time, saw only four persons put in a vote. So long
then as the eminent Junta can give us no official solution
of this enigma, we shall be compelled, by the evidence, to
maintain that the number 40,831 votes is a pure invention,
or that the votes were poured into the urns by the pailful.
We, therefore, call on the gentlemen of the ex-Junta, in
their own defence, and to satisfy a very natural curiosity on
the part of the Romans, to publish, if they can, the names,
both Christian and surname, of the 40,831 voters—all Romans."—*Il Divin Salvatore.*

This brings forcibly to my mind the language with which
Signor Lorente-Robaudi, Deputy for Nice, on the 12th of
April, 1860, protested before the House, against the value
of the impending plebiscitum of the people of Nice. "What
guarantees," he asked, "shall we have for the urns, when
they are taken to the Town Hall, and there left to remain
till to-morrow, under the care of those who want the separation from Italy? What guarantees will you give us that
these urns shall not be changed in the night for others full
of votes put there by an enemy's hand? And from such
votes as these, you are going to decide the nationality of a
country, our will to become Frenchmen instead of remaining what we are."

And three days later, he said of the vote already taken:

'Is it possible to get a vote in two or three days?' The Government, after having insulted Nice for many months, is now mocking it, and laughing at it. You cannot ask a country to vote, and arrange the electoral lists in two or three days. Europe cannot take such an act as the free vote of a free people."—*Official Acts of the Chamber, Nos.* 11 *and* 12. And if all this was true of the voting at Nice, where political feelings only would come into play, how much more true would it be of the voting at Rome and in the States of the Popes, where, not political feeling only, but the bitter hatred of revolutionists for authority and of infidels and apostates for the religion of Christ—the consciences of robbers fearing to lose the spoil they had seized, and the spite of traitors in their treason, would, all, contrive to make the returns they gave of an act registered only by themselves, doubtful and untrustworthy? And their own papers have been careful to tell us of the thousands of " emigrés," who came in the wake of the conquering army, to the city alone.* " Emigrés "—the sole title of most of whom to be Romans was the having once lived in the city, or the having come to prey on it in the sad days of the Revolution. It is notorious that this was the only claim to Roman citizenship which many Italian revolutionists could boast :—we have the official returns of political exiles ; and the population of Rome has, for the last few years, been steadily on the increase. They have told us, too, of the crowds that poured there for days before the Plebiscitum ; of the official leave to any *employés*, calling themselves " emigrés," to go to Rome to vote, free of cost, with a month's holiday and a month's pay. Then there is the testimony of foreign artists, who put votes into each urn of the city to test the worth of the vote ; there is the fact that the parish Registers were only

* These " emigrés " are given by their friends at numbers varying from 15,000 to 25,000. The *Times* correspondent at Florence was very particular and pathetic in describing the scenes at the railway station at Florence,—choked with " emigrés " for the few nights before the Plebiscitum came off.

6

taken from the churches the day before the Plebiscitum; the reports of eye-witnesses to the numbers of boys and lads who voted in the companies; and the fact, that nearly all the waiters in the cafés and hotels, the grooms and the domestic servants, are not Romans, but foreigners who come for the season, or for a few seasons, to live.

And now, if it be said, all this may be true; but the judgment of thoughtful Italians, of men moral and patriotic, has pronounced against the Temporal Power of the Popes, I reply, by referring you to an Appendix of quotations from the writings of men, in no case suspected, because they were in no sense partisans of the Pope-King. In their calmer moments these men have written as thoughtful men write. Weigh their words, I beseech you; and then turn to the table of the returns of the Italian Plebiscita, and judge how truly, or how falsely, the English public has been won to believe that Victor Emmanuel, King of Sardinia, is the elect of Italy; that Italian Unity, as he represents it, has been the dream or the desire of the Italian peoples.

I have the honour to be,   •

My Lords and Gentlemen,

Your Faithful Servant,

E. R. MARTIN.

Newnham Paddox, Lutterworth, Jan., 1871.

In order to give our readers some idea of the state of Italy as regards crime, during the year which has lately closed, we will give some statistics which will speak for themselves. They are taken from official sources, and it will be seen by them that never has Italy been in such a condition. As regards the money spent for the punishment or the prevention of crime it amounts to 45 millions of lire (about £1,781,250(, and yet, when compared with other European countries, there is a notable want of proper organisation in the prisons and penal arrangements.

A large amount is spent in the surveillance exercised over vice ; for 1,712,394 lire (£67,786) are apportioned to this detail, while 1,050,000 lire (£41,562) are employed as secret (service money by the Ministry of the Interior, and are chiefly employed in paying spies.

By the side of this how much is spent in works of charity and benevolence ? 20,858 lire (£825) ! and yet 30,000 lire (£1,187), and even 50,000 (£1,979) can be offered as premiums for the best designs for the House of Parliament !

We will now pass in review the frightful list of crimes and criminals. As regards murder and deeds of violence, there were during the first nine months of 1881, 2,318 murders and homicides, 164 infanticides, 27,251 offences of cutting and wounding, 1,222 highway robberies. This is stated to be an improvement upon the corresponding nine months of 1880, but, nevertheless, the figures are appalling.

Next come robberies and thefts. Of these there were 311 robberies with violence, 46,328 thefts of more or less magnitude, in town and country ; and the losses occasioned by cheating, undue appropriation, incendiarisms, destruction of animals and other property, amounts in the nine months to 8,386,235 lire (£331,955). As regards vice, up to July 1st, 1881, there were 10,491 names inscribed on the register of the health offices, of which 6,567 inhabited public houses of ill-fame, and 3,924 inhabited private houses. Out of these 1,951 had taken to evil courses through want, 356 at the instigation or through the corruption of their own families, 959 through desertion on the part of their husbands, 472 through love of luxury, and 2,548 through thorough depravation.

Also there exist in Italy 1,112 houses of ill-fame of variousclasses ; and the revenues arising from these, as recorded in the health officers' books for 1880 amounted to 591,985,20 lire (£23,432), and during the first six months of 1881 to 292,984,21 lire (£11,597). As for the streets 7,486 sick persons were found there, as well as 3,887 wounded or maltreated ; 813 dead (in this catalogue are comprised 123 victims of the Casamicciola disaster), 5,792 drunken men, 1,844 children deserted by their parents, 15,502 beggars. There were 1,919 vagrants under age taken up during the first nine months of 1881, and out of these, 1,846 were restored to their relations or guardians, and 535 were shut up in a public industrial establishment. Up to July 1, 1881, 65,905 were admonished or reprimanded, ot whom 22,026 were guilty of idleness and vagabondage, 12,551 of agrarian thefts, whilst 31,325 were suspected of crimes against property. Of these 7,231 were under age. There were also 8,505 men, 393 women, and 648 minors (8,898 in all) subjected to special surveillance, as well as 2,054 men, 12 women, and 46 minors confined to domicile, of whom the greater number were mechanics.

Strictly speaking there are no longer any convents or monasteries in Italy, but in their place there are 105,510 taverns and wine-houses, 21,512 beer and liquor shops, 23,548 cafés.

Many churches in Italy have been destroyed or converted to profane uses, but to compensate for this there are 14 first-class theatres, 72 second-class, and 1,049 third-class. The representations given from July 1st, 1880 to June 30th, 1881, amounted to 57,338, and yielded the Government 611,655,09 lire (£24,211). We may gather how many *freed* Italians abandon their country by the number of foreign passports given between July 1st, 1880, and June 20th, 1881. A passport is generally given for the whole family, and within the above period 49,091 were issued. The general directions chosen by both individual emigrants and families were America, France, and Africa.

All these figures are taken from Parliamentary documents, and give an idea of the state of morals in Italy of the present day. The greater number of the delinquents have almost from their birth been fanned by

82

Foreign Stocks are in considerable discredit, and as the nations continue to borrow heavily, and to spend more than their income, th discredit will increase. The wealth and capital of England is increasing yearly and the difficulty is to find good investments for capital at hom Tramways in large and populous districts are now offering good a apparently secure investments. It is calculated that for 5d. a mile, even less, an engine can be run. Iron rails are being laid down most towns. The only question, and it is a most important one in ea case, is, can the managers and directors of the company be trusted, n for honesty only, but for good and certain business habits?

taken from the
reports of eye-
who voted in t
the waiters in
domestic servai
for the season, i
And now, if :
ment of though
pronounced ag
reply, by referr
the writings of
in no sense pi
moments these
Weigh their wc
table of the ret
truly, or how
believe that Vic
of Italy; that
the dream or th

I

Newnham Pad

AUSTRALIAN FINANCE.

	Public Debt on the 31st Dec. 1880.	Public Debt per head.			Public Revenue per head. 1880.			Taxati per head 188c
	£	£	s	d	£	s	d	£ s
Victoria	22,060,749	25	16	9	5	8	3	1 19 7
New South Wales	14,933,919	19	17	0¼	6	10	7¾	1 17 9
Queensland.........	12,192,150	55	17	8¾	7	7	9½	2 15 c
South Australia ...	9,865,500	34	9	4¾	7	1	8½	1 17 c
West Australia ...	361,000	11	12	10½	5	16	2	3 5 3
Total Australia ...	59,383,318	27	12	9½	6	4	2½	2 0 4
Tasmania	1,943,700	16	15	11¾	3	16	0¼	2 12 7
New Zealand......	28,583,231	53	10	0¼	6	2	11	2 17 6
Total Australasia	89,910,249	32	2	6¾	6	1	11¾	2 4 :

Upon this a contemporary remarks that from the above table it v be seen that the public debt of Australasia averages over £32 per h of population, but the average for New Zealand is £53 10s. It generally considered that England is a heavily taxed and a hea indebted country, but were the National Debt of Great Britain to proportionate to that of Australasia it would amount to o £1,000,000,000. The Revenue raised in Great Britain is considera under £2 10s. per head, but in Australia taxation in one form or anot reaches over £6 per head. This heavy tax is borne with difficulty, : should the various Governments borrow further to any great exte there will be difficulty in several instances in providing funds to ca on the Government and meet the interest on the debts. It should borne in mind by investors that the necessities of the Government n always have precedence of the bondholders, so that unless the Reve is in excess of the necessities of the executive, there will be noth to pay interest with.

The most glaring case of over-spending is that of New Zeala This Colony has borrowed in a very few years the sum of £28,583, or £53 10s. per head of population, and it is with the greatest diffic that the Government can make both ends meet and pay the interes the debt.

During the month of November the Public Debt of the United St was reduced by 7,000,000 dols.

severalty. Are not tl he wild theories attempting ride the Red Horse (Apocal. vi., 4) and to take peace from the ear and to destroy one another? Suppose a million armed Chiname Kalmuc Tarters, and Afghans to land at Cork and claim their sha of the land in Ireland "as children of men" under the said title, wh would be the consequence? A violent collision would, no doul ensue, and be followed by as murderous a warfare at least as is report to exist in Ireland. Clearly the title to the land would have to settled by club law and gunpowder. Ireland is said to belong to t Irish, and ought, therefore, now to be divided among them grat share and share alike. But who are the Irish? It is clear that the is not a pure Irishman or Irishwoman in all Ireland. If a man c prove himself to be a pure, unadulterated Irishman he may make fortune by travelling about the country and shewing himself as a natu

APPENDIX.

I.

PIETRO VERRI—Voltairian—writes:—"The ruin of Papal Rome is a great loss for Italy, for with her we lose all influence in Europe, and each of us loses a common country, in which we were allowed to make our fortune."—*Scritti Varii*, vol ii. p. 54.

Ugo Foscolo—a bitter priest-hater—"We, Italians, desire, and ought to desire it to the last drop of our blood, that the Pope, a Sovereign, the Supreme Guardian of the religion of Europe, an Elective and an Italian Prince, should not only continue to reign, but *reign always in Italy*, defended by Italians."—*Discorso 2ndo. sulla servitù d'Italia.*

"People have forgotten the supernatural strength and the political wisdom of that grand Pontiff (Gregory VII.), who saw that the temporal dignity of the Church consisted in the independence of our cities; that in their confederation, the pastors of those cities found their most trusty defence." —*Discorso 3rzo.*

Bianchi-Giovini—a bitter priest-hater—"The Pope is the head of religion, and of a political state. Now he cannot discharge his chief duty worthily unless he is free, and unless he lives in a country *free from all external influence.*"—*Notes on Cormenin*, 55.

Carlo Botta—Historian:—"The thought of making the Popes wanderers, and, perhaps, also, First Almoners of the Emperors, was born at Paris. They were to have become Popes of *France*, not of *Christianity.—Storia d'Italia*, xxv.

Carlo Denina—Historian:—"The Cardinals and other subjects who form the Councils and the Tribunals of the Popes, only arrive at those posts through study, good conduct, and that distinguished merit which is comprehended by the term 'noblest' (*aristos*). They may rise to them from the lowest condition in birth; and hence it results that the system of that Government is democratic and popular. And as there is no nation excluded from the dignity of the Cardinalate, or even from the Papal dignity, Rome, by its Constitution, is the true country of cosmopolites."—*Storia d'Italia,* xxv. 9.

Leopold Galeotti :—" The Temporal Sovereignty guarantees the independence of the Papacy, in the same way as the possession of property and income guarantee the liberty of the Church. It guarantees it—because it saves the highest priestly power from being tyrannized over by the civil power. It guarantees it because it saves that power of arbitrating, which the Pope possesses, from the underhand influence of political quarrels. And, lastly, it guarantees it—because it saves the decrees of the Popes from the suspicion of being meant to offend the dignity which each Christian nation has a claim to."

" If the Pope had stayed at Avignon, he would have become Grand Almoner of France ; and out of France no other nation would have recognized him. A Pope, who was a subject of Charles V., could never have been accepted by Francis I. as umpire of peace. A Pope, who was a subject of Napoleon, would have become a dignitary of the French Empire. A Pope, who was a subject of the house of Austria, would neither be obeyed on the banks of the Vistula, nor on the banks of the Seine. It is of no use to argue that *Treaties and political Conventions would be sufficient to guarantee* the independence of the Pope. Treaties could, of course, declare that the Pope was theoretically independent of every civil principality. Diplomatic Conventions could equally remove the sacred person of the Pope and his Court beyond any sort of subjection. But neither Treaties nor Conventions *could change the reality of facts,* much less could they weaken the force of opinion, before which the one and the other would be equally impotent. The mere suspicion of a secret influence and of an underhand inspiration, *would destroy for ever all veneration, all reverence, and all confidence.* And suspicion, whether it comes down from palaces, or springs from the gutter, is the most desolating of the evil spirits which destroy human societies."— *Della Sovranita de' Papi,* 153.

Carlo Buoncompagni—Minister and Senator of the New Kingdom :—".The temporal power of the Popes had its rise in the efforts of the Roman Pentapolis to free itself from the rule of the Iconoclast Greek Emperors. It was confirmed by the veneration which the people had for the protection which the Roman Pontiff—Head of the Bishops—exercised, like all the other Bishops, to the advantáge of the Latin race; it was increased by the sensible policy of Charlemagne; it received new vigour from the Guelph party, which in the conflicts of the middle ages was rightly looked on as the party of the national interests in Italy; it became splendid by the light of the sciences and the arts, which had their chief seat at Rome."—*Rivista Contemporaneo;* vii.

Manzoni and Cesare Balbo are cited in proof of this statement. A little before he had said:—" It was not hateful to the people, for the powerful force of custom and tradition recommended it, as did the grand memories of Christian Rome, which *allowed no master there but the Pope.* It was recommended also by the virtues of most of the Pontiffs and of many prelates; by the *essentially gentle and pacific character* of the Government; by the liberality with which it protected the arts and several branches of intellectual culture; by the riches which flowed thitherwards from all the dioceses of the Catholic world, which made the burdens of its subjects few; and by the broad municipal liberties of the provinces.

Gino Capponi—Senator:—" The outrages endured by Boniface VIII., the stay at Avignon, and the forty years of schism, showed the Popes that it was more than ever necessary to guard the independence of the Church by the temporal sovereignty, and to make themselves like other princes."—*Archivio Storico,* i., 356.

Vincenzo Gioberti—Apostate Priest, Minister of the Kingdom of Sardinia:—" The Principality of the Pontiffs is one of the *most legitimate* in the world, for it has had its rise in the free consent of the peoples over whom it rules, and flourished morally long before it took the shape of a civil power."

Pietro Giordani—another Liberal—thus spoke in an oration before the Academy of Fine Arts at Bologna in 1815:—
" The older among us recollect the *quiet, the abundance, the security, the flourishing state of studies, the happy feast days, the delights of that pacific and blessed rule of the Pope,* when the lands were cultivated for the citizens—not for the prince; when the luxurious fruits of the lands went to render them still more fertile, more healthy, and more pleasant,—not to support soldiers; when commerce, unrestrained as it was, enriched the citizens—not the exchequer; and when the riches produced by commerce, did not go to beau-

tify the palaces, but our streets, our temples, our houses, and
our towns; when honest labour was rewarded and held in
honour, and poverty assisted ; and when words were not
dangerous for him who spoke them, and deeds were measured
by their just merit. And the older among us, remembering
always that happy time, were longing and desiring that those
bright days should return to so fair a district of Italy. Our
young people—more than half of us now living,—reared
amidst the noise and bloodshed of arms; when laws,
opinions, and governments are so loud and so voluble, knows
that as yet there has been no civil existence which could
last, or which one could wish should last. And it willingly
believes our fathers, who have tested it, that the Government
under which these lived so contentedly, must bring with it
every prosperity ; it willingly hopes that its present renown
will continue to posterity. And good reason have both the
old generation and the new to hope all this.

" For other Princes have of necessity many occupations,
many pleasures, that interrupt the task of pursuing only the
good of their subjects. But our Prince ought not to love war,
not to seek conquest. The pleasures of the chase, love, shows,
banquets, feasting, idleness, do not suit with his character.
Nothing else can please him but the governing his people so
lovingly and so wisely, that they may be the envy of every
other nation; in this alone can he find his delight, and this
is the only glory he can desire. What more shall I say ?
There are times when religion disturbs the feeble intellect
of Princes, and, with very grave loss to the people, puts
them in the clutches of hypocrites. But in the Supreme
Pontiff, religion can never become superstition, for he knows
it better than others know it; and he is the Sovereign
Teacher of it to all men. How then can it be that our common hopes should not be fulfilled by our common father ? "

This oration was printed, sold all over the country, " bought
up," writes the author, " by the people as by one man, for it
speaks the public mind." The original of the extract is in
my possession.

And Napoleon I. said, according to M. Thiers :—" The Pope
is a foreign Sovereign, and many people find fault with this
arrangement. But strange as it is, we must thank Heaven
it is so. What, in fact, could be so great an authority before
the power of the State ? United to the civil power, it would
be the despotism of the Sultan ; separated from it and
probably hostile to it, it would produce a terrible and intoler-

able rivalry. The Pope is not at Paris, and this is a good thing. We put up with his spiritual authority, really because he is neither at Madrid nor at Vienna. At Vienna and Madrid, they say the same thing. We are glad that he does not live with us, and that he does not live with our rivals, but at old Rome, far from the German Emperors, far from the King of France, and the King of Spain, holding the balance between Catholic sovereigns, yielding ever so little to the stronger, and then rising up against him as soon as he turns oppressor. The ages have consummated this work, and the ages have done well. This is, in fact, *the best and most beneficent institution for governing souls that one can possibly imagine.*"

Italy is, at this moment, a great Power. Sardinia and Naples were small ones when these writers wrote—when these thinkers thought. Is there one word of the independence of the Pope which does not apply to the case of an Italian Kingdom as it did of a French, a German, or a Spanish dominion ? And even more ; because the Popes are Italians by birth, and would be living in the very centre of the political web of Italy.

II.

The following are the official returns of the eight Plebiscita by which the kingdom of Italy was constituted :—

Rome	133,681
Venice	641,758
Tuscany	366,571
Emilia . . , . .	426,006
Naples	1,302,064
Sicily	432,059
The Marches	133,807
Umbria	97,040
Total . .	3,532,986

The population of Italy is broadly set down at twenty-six millions, being really in excess of that number. Subtracting five millions from the sum total for the ancient kingdom of Sardinia, and under three millions for Lombardy, there will still be, in the more than eighteen millions left, a large gap between the actual returns of the Plebiscita and the male population ; and the male part of the

population exceeds the female. We have, also, to remember
the very untrustworthy nature of these returns; the
absence of guarantees for age or country; the fact, asserted
by those who actually did it at the late Roman Plebiscitum, that foreigners could get voting tickets for each urn
in succession; and the strong suspicion that, as in the
Roman Plebiscitum of 1849—the Italianist Minister Farini himself being the witness—the votes were altered,
changed, and otherwise tampered with, by the interested
parties who had charge of the returns. We have seen how impossible it is to make those returns tally with the time of voting, the number of urns, and the actual concourse of the voters.
And it must be borne in mind that the will of the Piedmontese to absorb Italy, or of the Lombards to become part
of a great nation, could not reasonably affect the wills of
the remainder of the Italians. The truth, however, is that,
in Piedmont, there is a large proportion of educated people,
to say nothing of the uneducated, who would prefer the old
Kingdom of Sardinia to the great Kingdom of Italy; and,
in Lombardy, there are many who have accepted their fate
with comparative resignation, only since the downfall of
Austria, and the suicidal policy of Count Beust, have
made union with the old country little more enviable than
union with the Kingdom of Italy.

III.

The interest which the "regenerated" Italians take in
political life, Constitutional Government, and the delights of
a Parliament, may be gathered from the following figures—
at basis official. They are also instructive, because they
show how very little part the people take in the election of
Members of Parliament. The electoral lists have, in fact,
been compiled upon a principle of omitting objectionable
citizens, wherever it was possible to do so without too glaring a publicity. In the Romagna, hardly a tenth of the
people were allowed the franchise, at the election of the first
United Parliament. Two thirds of those who had it, refused
to have anything to do with elections conducted wholly by
the authorities of the Government. In the city and district
of Florence, less than half the number of those who had the
suffrage, voted; and the Members returned were, in fact,
returned by less than *a third.* So again at Lucca; while at

Pisa, only just over half voted; at Leghorn, was the same result; and at Arezzo, little over one third voted. Strictly speaking, the Duchy of Modena should have given 72,000 votes, it actually gave only 4,000. Yet, the first Italian Parliament was a great era in the history of Italy; we were told that the Italian people were wild with enthusiasm.

Ten years more, and the nation was completed by the possession of that Rome for which it had thirsted so ardently. Moreover, by this time, the nation was used to liberty and Parliamentary Government; and had learned to know that it was free. On the 20th November, 1870, a new Parliament was elected to ratify that possession of Rome—to sit, the first of all Italian Parliaments, on the Capitol. Imagine the first Irish Parliament, after a repeal of the Union, then look at the meagre result of Italian Unity, in the very moment of the supposed triumph of that unity.

On that day, 149 of the new members were elected for various parts of the kingdom. The actual number of voters whom these were supposed to represent—that is, the actual number having the franchise in the constituencies they represented—was 184,658; the actual voters were 61,240. Allow for a few odd votes not included, and one may still take a stand upon the fact that, in this supreme moment of the fate of Italy, only *one third* of the electors in 149 constituencies of Italy came forward to return members to Parliament. And of these we find the great cities of the kingdom thus represented :—

Place.	Members returned.	With the franchise.	Votes.
Florence . .	4	10,879	1,913
Milan . .	5	10,249	3,571
Naples . .	12	12,198	3,082
Turin . .	4	5,724	1,885
Genoa . .	4	4,177	1,068
Bologna . .	3	4,942	1,438
Venice . .	3	4,273	1,812

In only ten out of these 149 constituencies, did the voting interest half the persons who had the franchise; in the other cases the votes were only a third, a fourth, a fifth, and even a sixth of the number on the books. As a rule, the larger the town the fewer the votes; and the places with the largest number of votes were either in Piedmont, or especially Ministerial centres. Two places, with

660 and 944 electors respectively, sent members elected by 68 and 63 electors. The electoral returns of the city of Rome show nine candidates chosen by 2,060 voters, five of whom only would be the real representatives of the city, and would represent, therefore, a very small portion of the people, in a city of, ordinarily, over 200,000 inhabitants. And votes of this kind are very dependable evidence ; for the elections are, as a rule, conducted with proper regard to formalities, and the elector has only to ask for his voting ticket, and decide for which of the two candidates he will vote. So that, when we read that the Minister Sella is returned by 287 votes for a constituency of 1,379 electors ; that Ricasoli comes in by 412 votes for a constituency of 2,519 electors, and Peruzzi with 473 votes out of 2924, we can hardly be expected to have much belief in the parliamentary spirit of the " regenerated " Italians. And, here, it may be useful to quote from the Italianist *Romano* of the 16th November, which says of the public spirit at the election of the communal officers of the " newly regenerated " state of the Pope :—

" In some communes not a single elector came to vote ; the urns were deserted. In one village near Orvieto *two* came up ; in another *five*. Our legislators will have something to think of in this new fact."

From this abstention of the Romans, for what ought naturally, as nearest home, to interest them most, we may gather how little interest was felt in the election of Members of Parliament by these latest " regenerated " of Italians.*

* The ultra-Italianist *Diritto* of Florence—Jan. 9, 1871—says on this matter :—" The scandalous indifference of the electors in discharging their duties, of which, in the recent elections, we had so very humiliating a proof, raises the question how is it possible to cure this *gangrene which threatens our free Government in its very organism.*

LONDON : R. WASHBOURNE, PRINTER, 18A, PATERNOSTER ROW.